PROBLEM SOLVING FOR EVERY PROBLEM

THE PROBLEM SOLVER'S MANUAL TO FACE ANY CHALLENGES AND HANDLE LIFE'S HICCUPS

CONTENTS

INTRODUCTION

In 2015, researchers reported an unusual archaeological find that predates the pyramids of ancient Egypt. The seemingly unremarkable stones are the world's oldest stone tools dating back 3.3 million years. They predate any tools hitherto discovered by 700,000 years and are even older than the earliest humans. The Homo genus, to which we trace our roots, appeared no earlier than 2.4 million years ago. The tools must have been made by more ancient species, either the

Australopithecus afarensis or *Kenyanthropus platyops.*[1]

Our untrained eyes may not discern it, but the tools consisted of three types. Stone flakes are sharp-edged pieces "knapped" (or intentionally sheared off and not accidentally fractured) from larger rocks. Flakes were used for cutting, while other tools were used as hammers and anvils, the latter being larger and weighing as much as 15 kilograms. The anvils probably rested on the site, while other stones were smashed against it to make tools.[2]

It is not surprising that a genus preceding Homo created tools. Many primates are known to use tools intelligently. Chimpanzees, humanity's closest living relatives, habitually use makeshift hammers, spears, and other specialized tools without human help. Gorillas, the largest primates, use branches as walking sticks to test water depth and trunks to make bridges. They demonstrate the use of tools not only to find food but also to deal with their surroundings. [3]

Macaques living near Buddhist temples are known to pull hair from visitors to use as floss to clean their teeth. Mother macaques have been observed to slow down their motions to "educate" their young while passing the hair strands back and forth between their teeth. Orangutans have improvised whistles from bundles of leaves to signal the presence of danger to their family members. This marks the first time an animal has been known to fashion a tool to communicate. Since this knowledge is passed along to younger generations, it also exemplifies that culture – the passing of knowledge from one generation to the next – is not exclusive to humans.[4]

Tools are not the exclusive purview of primates. Elephants have been known to intentionally drop logs or rocks on electric fences to short them out. They also chew bark into balls to plug water holes to keep other animals from drinking them dry.

Asian elephants have systematically modified tree branches by breaking them down to ideal lengths to swat the flies alighting on them.[5]

Like land animals, ocean creatures also use tools. Sea otters use stones to hammer abalone shells on rocks, cracking open the hardest shells of their prey to eat the succulent meat inside. Dolphins have been known to carry marine sponges in their beaks to stir the sand at the ocean's bottom to uncover their prey. Octopuses use coconut shells as portable armor. They even stack up the shells and, sitting atop them while using their tentacles as stilts, transport them across the seafloor to use as shelter when needed.[6]

What does it mean for a creature to intentionally fashion tools to serve a specific purpose? We can only infer that the tool-making creature is capable of solving problems. It possesses the cognitive abilities to identify a need, to realize that its present situation cannot meet this need, and to modify something in its surroundings to satisfy its need.

Problems have beset us (and other creatures) since time immemorial. They exist as obstacles to our continued survival and prosperity. Species unable to eliminate these obstacles will likely face deterioration and eventual extinction, as many already have. Those that overcome ever-increasing hurdles evolve onto higher-order levels.

The same is true of our contemporary social order. Those among us who best solve problems are rewarded with the fruits of society, such as wealth, respect, renown, and positions of privilege. Those who fail at solving problems are compelled to rely on the charity and residue of the successful. If we are to improve our lot and the future of our descendants, we need to surmount our problems with a higher rate of success than our predecessors.

This book is intended as a manual of sorts that we may return to now and then to find ideas with which to address our problems. The first two chapters explain the fundamentals of the problem-solving process and the psychological dynamics in addressing our dilemmas. The third chapter provides a glimpse into the lives of outstanding individuals whose approaches to solving problems are worthy of emulation. The fourth chapter clarifies some problem-solving myths, and the fifth chapter describes the fundamental problem-solving methods.

The sixth chapter explains how costs and benefits are analyzed to solve problems. The walk-through example incorporated here will be a helpful guide for readers meeting this for the first time and a helpful recall tool for decision-makers already familiar with it. The seventh chapter lists and expounds on popular problem-solving frameworks as well as a problem-solving paradigm upon which we could pattern our solutions. The final chapter leaves us with some useful problem-solving tips.

A wealth of experience addressing a wide range of challenges imbues the chapters you are about to read. For over forty years, I have worked as an engineer, legal researcher, financial adviser, and university professor. I supervised workers and managed organizations, as well as raised children and ran a household. Intense research augmented the insights garnered from these experiences, all to create a book that is practical, engaging, and attuned to your needs.

If you are ready to become a better problem-solver, then turn the page, and enjoy the journey.

Dianna Gene P. Aquino

For Arlyne, Rey, Ramon, and Alvin

1

IT'S HUMAN NATURE – THE HUMAN RESPONSE TO DIFFERENT PROBLEMS

Every family has a drama queen, and in our family, the distinction fittingly goes to Nikki. As an adolescent, she was the temperamental one in the family. She once burst out in her characteristic wail: "Oh, dear God, I am so stressed! Math test, ballet practice, French class, art contest, and Rissa invited the gang for a sleepover tonight. Why, oh why, does everything have to happen at the same time?"

Arnold burst out laughing as he caught my eye roll, then turned to his younger sister. "Nix, I have a lot of work to do, too, just like you – except for the sleepover. That's girls' stuff." Then, trying to be helpful, he suggested: "Why not skip that? Then you have less to do." Nikki replied exasperatedly, "I can't. The girls who will be there will talk about the girls who won't be there!"

"Well," Arnold shrugged, "I'm glad I don't have your problems. But we all have problems. We just handle them differently."

"Your brother is right," I intervened. "Nikki, you don't have a problem with your activities because you enjoy doing them. You have a problem with managing the time to do them."

When Benjamin Franklin wrote in 1789, "Nothing is certain except death and taxes," he left out one thing: problems. Throughout our lifetimes, we encounter situations we find discomfiting because they challenge our comfort zone. Problems create stress that prompts us to act to resolve the problem. In doing so, we achieve mental acuity and emotional maturity in the process. Overcoming problems in our youth builds our resiliency to face more serious problems in adulthood. Encountering problems is a healthy part of life.

Problem And Its Definition

We spoke of problems as undesirable situations. In psychology, a problem is defined as an interactive relation between a subject and its surroundings, characterized by a conflict that the subject solves by searching for a transition from the initial condition to the final condition.[1] Thinking of a problem as a relation is strange to many of us, but it helps us to identify the interrelated elements in the conflict situation, like Nikki realizing that her problem involved the time element.

The "problematic relation" refers to one of two things:

1. A conflict between two contradictory tendencies the subject sees as incompatible, or a difference between the current situation and the aim the subject needs to achieve; or

2. A disorder in the objective situation or in the structure of activity and subjective uncertainty that causes activating tension and motivating focus.[2]

So, the relation described as problematic is incompatibility or disorder between two states, one of which is naturally desirable and the other undesirable. The presence of this conflict creates a tension (stress) that motivates us to act to restore compatibility between the current and desired situation.

The incompatibility may be simple and easy to remedy. For instance, John needs to cross a river and travels to where a bridge is normally found. Unbeknownst to him, the bridge was damaged during the previous storm. The gap in the bridge may be small, in which case John may use some nearby planks to create a walkway that can help him cross safely to the other side. Or the bridge may be entirely washed out, requiring John to find an alternative such as a boat or another bridge further down the river to enable him to cross over.

In other instances, the incompatibility between the desired and problematic situations may be serious and difficult to remedy. Take two countries, Russia and Ukraine, that differ in their understanding of how they ought to relate to each other. The leaders of the two nations undertake a series of complicated negotiations to settle their differences diplomatically. Failing at this, they ultimately feel compelled to resort to the ultimate recourse – armed conflict. Unfortunately, this is the way ancient tribes or modern nations have settled their problems intermittently throughout history. But it is an extreme form of solving a problem.

Nations resolve their difference according to diplomacy and politics. On the other hand, people are governed by their psychological makeup, or cognitive styles, when reacting to problems they meet.

Action Steps

Try to recall past problems that you consider to be particularly difficult and contentious. Try to identify the "problematic relationship" between your environment and your goal that is a natural desire. Environment means society, family, your life, career, or occupation, whatever situation you contend with. Recall how you solved the problem, or if it is still outstanding, how you may likely address it.

Moving On

Now in their thirties, Arnold and Nikki look back at their teen years and laugh at what they then considered their earth-shattering problems. We probably all do. As we grow older, our problems commensurately grow in size and gravity. The next chapter will give us a glimpse of how psychological factors influence the way we solve problems.

Key Takeaways

- Problems are barriers to our goals, creating tension in us and motivating us to work towards their elimination.
- In psychology, problems are interactive relations between us and our surroundings. The incompatible relation prevents us from reaching what we naturally desire for ourselves.
- Problems among human groups, such as tribes and nations, are also due to incompatible relationships which they seek to resolve through diplomacy or, if unsuccessful, through armed conflict.

2

THE PSYCHOLOGY OF PROBLEM-SOLVING

If you choose to not deal with an issue, then you give up your right of control over the issue, and it will select the path of least resistance.

Susan Del Gatto[1]

People respond to problems in different ways depending on their cognitive styles. Cognitive styles refer to "a person's characteristic mode of perceiving, thinking, remembering, and problem-solving." [2] There are various theories on cognitive styles, any of which can be related to how we deal with problems.

Cognitive Styles

Keen[3] conducted an experiment that explored the implications of people's cognitive styles with their problem-solving practices. This model categorized cognitive styles based on the degree to which they leaned more towards, logic and reasoning (structured/factual) or feelings and intuition. It identifies five styles:[4]

1. Systematic style – People who operate with this style use a well-defined, step-by-step approach when approaching problems. They seek a programmatic approach or overall plan to solve a problem. They base their response on concrete facts, figures, and data, and tend to address problems by segments.

2. Intuitive style – Intuitive people use an unpredictable ordering of analytical steps when solving a problem. They rely principally on "experience patterns characterized by unverbalized hues or hunches" [5] as they explore and quickly abandon one alternative after another. They concentrate on ideas and feelings, and their response to the problem may be emotion-based, keeping the overall problem in mind rather than focusing on the situation in segments.

3. Integrated style – People with an integrated style are both systematic and intuitive, and can quickly and easily shift from one style to the other. They change styles unconsciously as the situation demands and project an energetic and proactive capability in solving problems. They develop a reputation as "problem seekers" due to their uncanny ability to identify potential problems and opportunities of finding better ways to do things.

4. Undifferentiated style – It seems that people with undifferentiated cognitive

behavior do not display any noticeable style (i.e., neither systematic nor intuitive). When undifferentiated people encounter a problem or learning situation, they exhibit receptivity to guidelines or instructions from outside sources rather than act according to their own initiative. They tend to be passive or withdrawn and reflective, looking to mimic others' problem-solving strategies.

5. Split style – People with a split style are situated in the middle range in both the systematic and intuitive scales, and have a fairly equal tendency towards both approaches. Initially, people with the split style may be confused as those with the integrated style. But people with the split style do not exhibit the integrated behavioral response of quickly changing from one style to the other. Rather, split-style people use only one style at a time, exhibiting each style in completely different settings depending on the nature of the task. While integrated people shift unconsciously, split-style people make the conscious response to select the style

appropriate to the problem or learning situation.

The experiment by Keen found that significant results related people's problem-solving behavior to three particular styles: the systematic and intuitive styles, which are the extreme opposites, and the integrated style which is a combination of both. She called people who employ the systematic style the "thinking type," and those who follow the intuitive style the "feeling type." By focusing on the two extremes, Keen[6] identified the problem-solving strengths of each according to the following table:

Thinking Type	Feeling Type
Analysis	Persuasion
Organization	Concentration
Weighing "the law and the evidence"	Teaching
	Forecasting how others will feel
Finding flaws in advance	Advertising
Holding consistently to a policy	Selling
	Appreciating others' thinking
Reforming what needs reforming	
Standing against opposition	

Comparing the strengths of the cognitive styles represented by the thinking and the feeling types, we can readily describe the type of problems, and problem-solving techniques, each style best addresses. The thinking type, or systematic style, is analytical and well-organized, best equipped to solve technical problems requiring a step-by-step procedure. The feeling type, or intuitive style, is impulsive and directed by impression, best attuned to problems involving people and social situations. When people face problems that appeal most to their cognitive styles, they are productive and happy.

Rarely, however, do we work alone since modern working and living conditions require us to work with others. If in a business organization, workers are organized into specialized units where they collaborate with others like themselves, then there is general harmony because members of the same team communicate well with each other and have the same thinking style. Engineers in the technical department communicate well and work systematically with each other. Artists in the product design department will likewise collaborate more effectively by applying more intuitive processes.

But when workers with divergent cognitive styles are forced to work together without careful managerial supervision, the incompatibilities between workers' thinking styles may create more problems than are solved. Consider the following case.

Thomas and Stella worked at a sports shoe manufacturing company called the Rubber World Company. Stella is a product design team leader and Thomas is head of production engineering. Stella was assigned to come up with a novel design for kids' rubber shoes, the first ever kids' shoes the company will produce. Thomas was tasked to design the production system that included the cutting, sewing, and polyvinyl chloride (PVC) injection process. He was also required to specify the machinery needed as well as the workers – the cutters, sewers, and machinists – for the new product. Thomas will organize his production line depending on the final product design Stella's team will produce.

Based on their customer survey and market study, Stella's team came up with a shoe design that was a delight to see. The shoe's upper, which consists of the part of the shoe that covers the top and sides of the foot, was multicolored and had several decals that improved the shoe texture. Popular cartoon characters also enhanced the design and made it more attractive to the little children who were its target market.

When Stella forwarded the prototype of the new product design to Thomas' team, a collective gasp was audible from the production team.

Figure 2.1 - Kids' rubber shoes[7]

The shoe design was a production team's nightmare. Cutters will have to cut each decal as a separate piece, which sewers will need to attach to the shoes' uppers individually. Each color in the PVC portions will need a separate injection process which will need a separate set of molds or additional machines, with each machine costing hundreds of thousands of dollars. The entire process will involve more material, machinery, and manpower – and consequently, more money – than management allocated to the production team. Take a look at a shoe structure online to get a hint of the design's complexity.[8]

This case is an example of two thinking styles conflicting in solving a problem. Stella, an intuitive thinker, created a design based on little regard for the production aspect. Thomas, a systematic thinker, wanted a simple design to reduce the cost and complexity of production without regard for the target consumers' tastes and preferences. In such a situation, higher management will need to step in and negotiate a happy compromise between the two teams.

People Who Are Most Prone To Problems

Keen's experiment did not set out to identify which among the thinking styles is more prone to encounter problems. Realistically, all people, bar none, have their share of problems. They just differ in type and complexity. Keen's experiment aimed to discover the sources of conflict people with different thinking styles encountered when they worked together to solve a problem.

The results of the experiment showed that people who have the same cognitive styles solve problems more smoothly when they work together. People who easily switch styles - in this case, the integrated thinker - arrive at solutions to problems harmoniously with partners having different cognitive styles. But complications arise when intuitive and systematic thinkers try to solve problems together due to at least three differences in their working relationship.

First, they do not communicate well together, as intuitive thinkers convey their message in terms of feelings and sentiment, while systematic thinkers prefer to convey clearly defined facts and reasons. Second, they view the task in different contexts. The product development case involving Stella and Thomas is one example. The problem of developing a new product was viewed from an artistic context by Stella and a manufacturing context by Thomas without a specified middle ground. Third, differences in behavior tend to cause friction between the two styles. Intuitive thinkers are irritated by what they perceive to be slow, studied methods of systematic thinkers, while the latter are annoyed by the impulsive, seemingly carefree manner with which the former jump to conclusions.

How can we bridge these gaps in cognitive styles so that they do not add to the complexity of solving existing problems? The best strategy would be to target the three areas where these gaps exist – communication, context, and behavior. A manager who oversees subordinates with divergent cognitive styles who are tasked to work together must establish the proper parameters beforehand.

- Certain measures can shed greater light on co-workers' expectations of each other. These include setting up communication channels, periodic reports, and planning and brainstorming sessions scheduled at strategic intervals during the project's execution.
- Milestones should be discussed and agreed upon clarifying how progress is being made, and identifying obstacles and modifications so that team members may adjust their activities promptly.

- More importantly, personal interaction, including social meet-ups, can be encouraged so that colleagues may gain an understanding of how and why other members may think a certain way about the project.

The overall goal is to foster better collaboration among diverse team members, harness the benefits of both intuitive and systematic approaches, and arrive at the best solution possible.

Skills And Abilities That Aid Problem-Solving

Our cognitive styles determine how we think when we solve problems. Other than this, our skills and abilities also influence how effectively we arrive at solutions to our dilemmas. While our cognitive style may be hardwired to our minds such that we can do little to consciously change it, there is much we can do to acquire new skills and abilities, or at least hone what we already have. Psychological researchers have sought to link the following abilities and skills with problem-solving competence.

Intellectual Ability

Wenke and Frensch[9] defined intellectual ability as "the basic cognitive faculties, processes, and mechanisms that differ in degree among persons, affect performance on a wide variety of tasks, and are not modifiable by experience."[10] This definition includes all information-processing characteristics as potential intellectual abilities. A person's intelligence quotient (IQ) score is a measure of a person's intellectual ability.

With that operating definition, the authors conducted a series of experiments that did not find strong evidence that intellectual ability has a causal link with problem-solving competence. Simply stated, being a good problem solver is not caused by superior intellectual ability. The authors caution, however, that there might indeed be a link, but their investigation just cannot find proof of it. They discovered that complex problem-solving competence is associated with task knowledge and strategy, which may in turn be tied to intellectual ability.

Therefore, the fact that we may not be intellectually superior does not mean that we cannot be good problem-solvers. Many of us will find great comfort in that.

Creativity

Creativity, as conceptualized only since the beginning of the twentieth century, is "a skill that rises above the more traditional ways of thought" that forms uniquely original ideas.[11] Not all problems require a high level of creativity. There are "canned" problems or problems that require only established knowledge that is generally known. The hallmark of creative problems is that they involve breaking away from the conventional. In contrast to "canned" problems, "real" problems require new, never-before-tried ideas. That takes creativity, and since all canned problems began as real problems when they first emerged, then it does not strain credibility to say that all solutions begin with a spark of creativity.

There are a few problems we presently encounter that have not evolved through decades and even centuries, so we often have previous knowledge on which to build. But one clear exception was the problem of building a spacecraft to travel to and land on the moon when Apollo 11 was planned for in 1969. Before Apollo 11, only a handful of people had left the earth's atmosphere, and none had landed on another heavenly body. The lunar module was one of three parts of the Apollo 11 spacecraft which included the command and service modules. All three modules had their specific roles and needed to fit perfectly with each other hundreds of thousands of miles out in space.

The lunar module (LM) was envisioned to break away from the command module once it had reached the moon's orbit. It was to land safely on the moon's surface, and after the onsite activities were completed, launch from its base and reconnect with the service module for the trip back to earth. Tom Kelly, at the head of 8,000 engineers and technicians of the Grumman Corporation, developed the module from scratch. Starting with a blank canvas, Kelly and his team worked on the project 24 hours a day, seven days a week, for nearly a decade.[12] Eventually, they succeeded, with a great deal of industry and creativity.

The result was a machine unlike any other vehicle ever built before. It became the model for succeeding missions until Apollo 17, the last manned mission to the moon.

Figure 2.2 - Model of the Apollo 11 Lunar Lander Module, 'Eagle' [13]

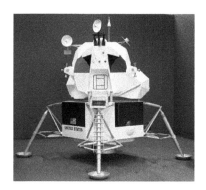

Loubart and Mouchiroud[14] state that creativity needs a diverse set of cognitive and conative factors. Cognitive factors involve conscious intellectual activity, while conative factors link knowledge to action.

Essential cognitive abilities include identifying and redefining the problem, recognizing information in the environment relevant to the problem, recognizing similarities between different fields that clarify the problem, metaphor, selective comparison, and combining these results to form a new idea, among other activities.

Conative factors focus on personality traits leading to motivation to action. More creative people have conative abilities such as assertiveness, independence, individualism, nonconformity, spontaneity, and lower socialization. The authors suggest that creative people must "defy the crowd" and take on risks to advance new ideas, but unfortunately, many are just too risk-averse which limits their creativity.

Overall, intrinsically-motivated problem-solvers are more innately creative because the achievement of the goal is the reward in itself. Extrinsically-motivated people look to external rewards to remain focused. Managers of these workers must provide a stimuli-rich physical environment for their subordinates while minimizing the negative effects of time constraints, competition, and unnecessary regulation, to promote creative problem-solving in the workplace.

Insights

The American Psychological Association (APA) defines Insight as "the clear and often sudden discernment of a solution to a problem by means that are not obvious and may never become so, even after one has tried hard to work out how one has arrived at a solution." [15]The APA's definition hints at the mystery behind the source of insight, something that research has not yet discovered. Davidson [16]observed that old knowledge, such as information stored in long-term memory, helps individuals view current problems in new ways – the definition of insightful problem-solving.

To date, all that is known about insight is that it is the sudden realization of a solution that appears correct.[17] Webb, et al. [18]notably concluded, however, that the subjective feeling of warmth and the *Aha!* or a strong feeling of insight are elicited when a correct solution is encountered. Thus, whatever "insight" might be, it is characterized by strong emotions of discovery and, possibly, delight, versus problem-solving arrived at principally through incremental logical steps.

Working Memory

Goldman-Rakic [19]described "working memory" as "the combination of moment-to-moment awareness and instant retrieval of archived information."[20] Cowan [21] contrasts working memory with long-term memory by characterizing the former as the minimal information held in the mind to execute cognitive tasks such as planning, comprehension, reasoning, and especially problem-solving. Working memory holds information for a short time – thus, short-term vis-à-vis long-term memory – because mental processes involve multiple steps with intermediate results a person must temporarily remember while accomplishing the task.

Relative to working memory, a problem can be seen as "a goal that is not immediately attainable."[22] For the length of time we need to attain that goal, working memory plays a vital role since it maintains memory representations in a state of high activation and accessibility. For instance, in the course of solving a problem, we might arrive at an impasse or obstacle. During this time, our mind pulls together previous multiple problem-solving attempts in search of a solution that overcomes the current deadlock. Thus, working memory capacity at this point must be sufficiently expanded to accommodate the process of comparing past results with the prevailing dilemma, or inhibit information that is not relevant.

The cognitive functioning that relates to working memory capacity during problem-solving is referred to as fluid intelligence. Fluid intelligence covers the aspects of cognition that are independent of prior knowledge and experience. It is measured with tests of abstract reasoning and spatial visualization that emphasize novel problem-solving. Research has established a strong correlation between working memory and fluid intelligence, particularly in three areas: verbal, spatial, and numerical.

Working memory capacity can also be involved in problem-solving difficulties. Working memory capacity represents the capability for controlled attention, which does two things: maintain information in a highly activated state, but also suppress irrelevant or misleading information.[23]

Supposing Tom Kelly, who headed the team that designed the Eagle, the Apollo 11 Lunar Module, was fixated on the earlier spacecraft he helped design for missions that orbited the earth. His reliance on such designs would have been irrelevant and misleading. Had Kelly been unable to inhibit this information, he would have failed to design a spacecraft built to land on the moon. This phenomenon, known as functional fixedness, is the inability to use familiar concepts in a novel manner. It, therefore, constrains working memory capacity from efficient problem-solving.

Working memory is not always needed for performance, only when maximum attention is needed to perform well when distractions are present. For instance, you are cooking your favorite meal, one you have whipped up many times before. You can do this half-attentively while watching a television show and talking to someone on your mobile phone. It is a task that does not demand your full attention, so you could accomplish it even with many distractions. But assume you are solving a difficult problem, such as figuring out your income tax return. Your working memory capacity will tend to shut off distractions such as the television and incoming phone calls until you finish the task.

Comprehension Of Text

Text comprehension refers to our ability to understand words. Imagine that you purchased a new laser printer from an online distributor, and the product arrived in its deconstructed form straight from the factory. You opened the cardboard packaging and the plastic casings housing the printer's components. These included cables, other attachments, and the ink cartridges which you were supposed to assemble. An instruction manual came with the machine, specifying the address to a website you can refer to in case you have concerns the manual does not address. You have not used this type of printer before, nor have you assembled one in the past.

If you had read through the manual and successfully assembled the printer based on the written instructions, then you are likely to have an excellent comprehension of the text. This is not a simple matter. It means you have accurately represented in your mind (1) the problem, and (2) the messages in the instruction manual. The text representation is "a cognitive representation that has some reference to elements, features, or structural patterns in the explicit text."[24] In solving certain problems, we must be able to build an accurate and integrated representation of the text relating to the problem.

If you recall high school algebra, you probably remember working through word problems. Lest you panic, we're not going to do one now. We'll simply consider a statement that includes some numbers:

"In an office, the human resources department found that 100% of the female employees are romantically involved with 2% of the male employees."

Should this be a cause for concern for the HR department, which is tasked with the enforcement of ethical behavior in the workplace? Some people will read quickly through the statement and gasp in horror at its impropriety. "What? One hundred women are romantically involved with two men?"

But those who have a keen comprehension of the text will be quick to pick up on the potentially misleading implication of percentages. If there were only two female employees and one hundred male employees in the office, then the two women comprise 100% of the female employees, and two of the men comprise 2% of the male employees. It is entirely proper that two women could be romantically related to two men in the office. The text representation of the "100% of females" and "2% of males" is cognitively interpreted to mean two couples.

Action Steps

Of the skills and abilities that we enumerated, the one that many people find challenging is creativity and how they could enhance their creative skills. Daisy Barringer [25] has some interesting exercises she recommends to increase this ability. We invite you to try three exercises we adapted from Barringer's list, described below.

1. Think of a six-word story.

This is a nod to Ernest Hemingway who wrote, "For sale: baby shoes, never worn." Just six words convey a sad story of frustrated parenthood. The challenge here is to condense the gist of a story into six words. Here's my attempt at it: "Pieces of people, come to life." Guess the Mary Shelley novel that inspired it.

2. Look at things from a new perspective.

My sixth-grade teacher gave us a story to read where a young man tragically loses his life. She then told us to retell the story, but from the point of view of the man who died. It was a challenge to get the character to tell the parts of the story after his death. Some therapists tell people in relationships to practice looking at events from the other person's point of view. Assuming a new perspective can turn our world around and give you fresh insight.

3. Write down the problem you are trying to answer.

How many times have you been mulling over a problem, and then discover that you left out an important detail that changed everything? Write the problem and all its details explicitly, and you might just discover a solution you might not have thought of before.

Moving On

The brain is the most complex organ in the human body. Our mind is more than just our brain: it is the very dwelling place of our personality. Everything about us is involved when we solve problems; this includes not only our thoughts but also our emotions and convictions. The next chapter will give us a glimpse of the really large problems that historical figures contended with, and how they overcame them.

Key Takeaways

- People respond to problems in different ways depending on their cognitive styles - systematic, intuitive, integrated, undifferentiated, or split.
- The two extreme cognitive styles define the two main problem-solving behaviors, namely the thinking type and the feeling type.
- People of dissimilar cognitive styles who work together are most prone to problems in the workplace. Co-workers' expectations of each other must be clarified before working together.
- Skills and abilities that aid problem-solving are intellectual ability, creativity, insights, working memory, and text comprehension.

3

HISTORICAL PROBLEMS AND THEIR GREAT SOLUTIONS

" We don't have to waste our time learning how to make pastry when we can use grandma's recipes.[1]

— ORSON DE WITT, *EARTH WON'T MISS YOU*

We learn a lot from our grandparents. My grandma, an English teacher, taught me a word difficult for a three-year-old. Maybe it was memorable because it was difficult. The word is *vicarious.* Vicarious experiences are others' experiences that we make our own. It means learning by imagining ourselves in others' shoes. Vicarious learning is the best way to learn, short of having our own experiences. That's probably why all children enjoy the stories told by their elders.

This chapter will give us a glimpse into the lives of some of history's best problem-solvers. They are people who have faced great challenges in their lives and overcame them. By learning their stories, we may gain some insight into how they confronted their problems and arrived at solutions that benefit not only themselves but the rest of mankind.

Albert Einstein

Probably no single scientist has contributed more to making space travel possible than Albert Einstein. But while the theory of relativity is the greatest and best-known achievement of this remarkable man, he has made numerous contributions that have led to many aspects of modern living. Einstein developed principles that were instrumental in bringing us paper towels, solar power, a method of forecasting stock market prices, and laser pointers, among other things.[2] All of these discoveries certainly began as a problem, which makes Einstein one of the great problem-solvers in history.

> If I had an hour to solve a problem, I'd spend 55 minutes thinking about the problem and five minutes thinking about solutions.[3]

— ALBERT EINSTEIN

Based on this quote, Einstein was of the notion that the key to solving a problem lies in thoroughly understanding the problem. Once we had done that, then the solution would readily present itself. If Einstein were precise about the time he would allocate to understand a problem (which is likely, given his affinity for math), then he would have typically spent 92% of the time understanding a problem and 8% solving it.

One day, as I parked the car in our garage, I forgot to engage the handbrake before I alighted from it. The car rolled down the slight incline and plowed into our flower box with a loud *ker-flump*. The dent on the fender looked nasty to me, so I was quietly calculating how much we would spend on an expensive body repair when my husband ran out of the house.

With the patience of a saint, Noel examined the extent of the damage. "Hmmm. The paint is intact. No breaks or scratches. Hmmm. Hmmm." He looked outside and under, ran his fingers through the offending indentation, reached for his mobile phone, and did some surfing. After what seemed a while, he went in and emerged with a hair dryer, some ice, and a pair of heavy-duty gloves.

He switched on the dryer and ran some hot air over the dent, then after a while applied the ice over it. The dented fender appeared to magically spring into shape with a distinct *pop!* Noel grinned at my astonished look. "All done!" The entire operation took no more than a minute. Exactly as Einstein described it.

Other quotations shed further light on Einstein's thinking regarding problem-solving. Consider the three following. The next reinforces his earlier admonition that we spend more time studying a problem

> It is not that I'm so smart, it's just that I stay with problems longer.

Remarkably, Einstein mentions no other qualifications or requirements, except for the time spent "staying with a problem." Other than time spent with honest effort, it would not take genius or intellect to ensure the success of a solution.

> The formulation of a problem is far more essential than its solution, which may be

merely a matter of mathematical or experimental skill. To raise new questions, new possibilities, to regard old problems from a new angle requires creative imagination and marks real advances in science.

Formulating a problem, in the sense Einstein meant, is not the superficial manifestation by which we recognize there is a problem. What we identify as the problem is often the manifestation; we need to find the cause. When physicians ask their patients, "What is the problem?" the patients describe what afflicts them: abdominal pain, fever, swelling, a lack of appetite, and so on. Doctors take note of the symptoms, but still have to identify, or formulate, the problem. The source of the symptom may be as simple as slight indigestion, or as serious as a life-threatening disease. Only after running tests and arriving at a diagnosis could the doctors formulate the problem by stating the cause of the affliction and constraints

within which the problem may be solved –
that is, how the patient may be healed.

66

> The problems that
> exist in this world can not be
> solved by the level of thinking that
> created them.

For a problem to be solved, new
knowledge must be gathered that
elevates the thinking process above that
in which the problem was created.
Everyone has experienced a situation
wherein the solution they came up with
complicates the problem and makes
things more difficult than they were
before. Raising our level of thinking is
also known by another buzzword:
"Thinking outside the box," also known as
lateral thinking. An exercise in lateral
thinking is awaiting you in the Action
Steps section of this chapter.

Finally, there is this from the Father of
Modern Physics:

66

When the solution is simple, God is answering.[4]

Although he may be the world's most revered 20th-century scientist and intellectual, Albert Einstein seemed to have acknowledged that not all solutions to problems can be explained away by the human mind. We should always allow for the possibility that the answers to some problems come unexplained.

Curtis LeMay

Curtis Emerson LeMay served as the Chief of Staff of the U.S. Air Force under two U.S. presidents, John Kennedy and Lyndon Johnson, but this is only one small part of his 37-year career. He became the youngest Major General not only in the Army Air Forces but also in the U.S. Army at the age of 37. At only 44 years old, he was also the youngest General since Ulysses S. Grant. For his outstanding service, he was awarded the

Distinguished Service Cross, Silver Star, three Distinguished Flying Crosses, and four Air Medals, aside from various other campaign medals and foreign accolades.[5]

The highly respected LeMay nevertheless was known among his men by other names. They referred to him as "The Cigar," "Iron Ass," "The Old Man," and "Bombs Away LeMay." The Japanese also called him "Kikhiku Rumei," which loosely translated as beast or monster, because of the Air Force's destruction of their industrial cities under his command. LeMay's honor was later vindicated, however, when Japan awarded him the Grand Cordon of the Order of the Rising Sun, First Class, for his work in reconstructing post-war Japan. The Grand Cordon is the second-highest honor that may be bestowed and conveys forgiveness and a change of heart from the war damages the nations inflicted on each other.[6]

How could such a man seem to manifest two divergent personalities, stern and ruthless at times but also beneficent and empathetic? Though he may appear uncompromising and tough, those who best knew him said he had a soft heart.[7] How one of his colleagues described him may shed light on how we should view this enigmatic man.

> LeMay, supposedly the meanest, toughest commander in the Eighth Air Force, actually allowed his men to say anything they damned pleased about anyone in the room, including himself. And he didn't argue with them. He sat there and listened until they were through.[8]

— COLONEL CARL NORCROSS

LeMay was known for his leadership qualities, but foremost of his managerial qualities was the way he solved problems. He was actively focused on figuring out how he may improve his organization to better the job done. As exemplified by Norcross's statement,

LeMay placed his emphasis on people. An example of the tough problems he faced was when, in 1942, he had no aircraft, equipment, or trained personnel, and was confronted with good men dying due to unreadiness. Since then, LeMay assumed the mindset of competence and constant preparedness that brought about a cultural change in the Strategic Air Command (SAC).[9] How he did this was nothing short of phenomenal.

> LeMay's reliance on the people he selected for senior positions [allowed] him time to be available on short notice. By concentrating on basic strategies and major decisions, while depending on his staff to formulate them, he escaped the trap of a bulging schedule that would have made mature planning difficult. As a result, he was able to stay in complete control of SAC's operations, while being one of the most available persons in the headquarters.[10]

LeMay, therefore, had a gift for personal leadership, coupled with an understanding of the organization and appreciation of his staff when crafting strategies for wartime missions. He understood that he could not solve a monumental problem by himself, but needed others to contribute with their well-trained skills towards finding a solution.

But most of all, General LeMay was keenly aware of the lessons of history. When his decision could cost the lives of men, he was careful to remember how the generations of leaders before him faced the same problems and dealt with them. Where there was failure, he resolved to avoid the same pitfalls. When there was victory, he was eager to learn from the same and improve upon it.

Few folks ever learn anything from previous experience of elders, whether elders in years or elders in familiarity with a given task or problem … No generation ever halts to turn around and examine the vast lore acquired by their predecessors who marched along the same route; and then to adjust a future plan (or a present crisis) accordingly. Instead, they criticize the previous generations for making severe errors—such obvious errors, in the light of modern technocracy and modern emancipated philosophy! Then they turn around and make a whole new set of mistakes all by their lonesome.[11]

— GENERAL CURTIS LEMAY

There is much we can learn from this stern but compassionate leader. When solving problems, look to the examples of the past and focus on the strength and insight of the people around you. LeMay's problem-solving philosophy guided him through the hard decisions that spelled the difference between life and death.

Genghis Khan

          His fame reached as far as England.

This noble king was called Genghis Khan

Who in his time was of so great renown

That there was nowhere in no region

So excellent a Lord in all things.[12]

— GEOFFREY CHAUCER

In this vignette, Chaucer, the renowned 14th-century English poet who preceded William Shakespeare, wrote of an excellent, renowned, and incomparably noble king named Genghis Khan. Interestingly, a contemporary article on the Internet described Genghis Khan as "a barbaric conqueror whose troops raped and murdered hundreds of thousands, if not millions, of people and pillaged and often destroyed villages, towns, and cities throughout Asia and Europe."[13]

If all you knew about Genghis Khan were the two descriptions above, you would have concluded, "Must've been two different Genghis Khans." To be fair, you could have easily said this of a person named John or Joan Smith, but honestly, nobody names their child Genghis Khan. Not even Genghis Khan's parents. He was named Temujin by his father, Yesugei, and only adopted the name Genghis in 1206 when he was proclaimed ruler or "Khan" at a meeting or "*kurultai*" of all the Mongolian tribes.[14]

Accepting that the quotations speak of one and the same Genghis Khan, how then do we reconcile the differences in perception? We do this by recognizing that the two descriptions are not mutually exclusive, nor are they complete characterizations of the man. The actions alleged by the Internet article were factual, and while they are horrific by today's standards, they were material in the successful creation of the Mongol empire, given the context of the period.

But we are not here to pass moral judgment on Khan based on presentism. Khan ruled over the largest contiguous empire in history,[15] which means that his problem-solving philosophy and methods yielded consistently effective results. This interests us because, albeit the disparity in standards of moral leadership over time, effective problem-solving throughout history is always measured by one standard: making the right decisions.

1. Genghis Khan did not let his limitations hinder him from realizing his destiny. The young Temujin had a difficult childhood. Before he turned 10, his father was poisoned to death by an enemy clan. Temujin's own clan deserted them, and his mother was compelled to raise seven children by herself. He was captured and enslaved by his clan, but he managed to escape.[16] He was illiterate, but he was a natural leader and born diplomat,

knowing instinctively how to deal with tribal chiefs.[17]

2. He let the best ideas win the day.[18] Although he was a ruthless conqueror, Khan demonstrated that he was an enlightened leader for his time. Life was pretty good for those who submitted to his rule. He allowed for the freedom of religion, abolished torture, eliminated aristocratic privilege, and established the rule of law. He ruled pragmatically and emphasized meritocracy. He drew the best ideas from everywhere, and combined systems drawn from other cultures; whatever worked best was implemented everywhere.

3. He embraced the diversity of his newly conquered territories. He was tolerant[19] and actively interested in the philosophies of other religions. He studied Islam, Buddhism, Taoism, and Christianity.[20] This served, at least in part, a political goal: tolerance to a culture's deepest-held beliefs kept the subjects happy, staving off the likelihood of rebellion. But Genghis Khan also had a personal

interest in spirituality. Khan was known to pray in his tent for days before important campaigns and met with the religious leaders of various denominations to discuss the details of their beliefs. At his advanced age, he had long conversations with the Taoist leader Qiu Chuji on immortality and philosophy.

4. He ruled wisely. He allowed the local leaders the administration of their respective territories. He also established a body of laws, Khan's Great Law, which relied largely on the customs and traditions of the various herding tribes, although when old practices hindered the functioning of his empire, he readily eliminated them. Groups were allowed to follow their traditional laws as long as they did not conflict with the Great Law. His rule paralleled the modern civil law norms in some ways.[21] Genghis Khan reasoned,

> People conquered on different sides of the lake should be ruled on different sides of the lake.[22]

Unlike other world conquerors, Khan never considered himself divine. Since he sought to unite the whole world, he applied the law to everyone, even himself. This was the first time in history that the ruler was also subject to the law since this was something no other civilization had yet done. [23]

5. He was a master tactician and organizer. He built roads and bridges, established communication networks, and created alliances. He installed one of the first international postal systems, a mounted courier service called the "Yam," which formed the backbone of the empire's vast communication network.[24] On the battlefield, he used siege warfare, spy networks, and supply routes with way stations to enhance the communication of secret intelligence.[25]

6. Some of his most trusted generals were former enemies.[26] Khan had a keen eye for good men and promoted his officers based on skill and experience rather than entitlement. One incident exemplifying this took place in 1201

during a battle against a Taijut tribe. Genghis Khan was almost killed when his horse was shot down from under him with an arrow. After the battle, he addressed the Taijut prisoners, demanding to know who was responsible for the incident. One soldier bravely admitted to the deed. Moved by the archer's boldness, Khan made him an officer in the army and gave him the moniker "*Jebe*" which meant "*Arrow*" to commemorate their first meeting on the battlefield. During the Mongols' subsequent conquests of Asia and Europe, Jebe became one of their greatest field commanders.

7. He left no issue unresolved and no score unsettled.[27] Every other kingdom he conquered, he gave a chance to submit peacefully to Mongol rule. But societies that resisted his orders felt the brunt of his wrath. One of his most famous acts of revenge took place in 1219 when the Shah of the Khwarezmid Empire violated a treaty with the Mongols. Khan offered him a valuable trade agreement to exchange goods along the Silk Road. Instead, the Shah

had his emissaries murdered. Enraged, Khan unleashed his hordes on the Khwarezmid territories in Persia and laid waste to the Shah's entire empire, murdering millions in the process.

There are many more attributes of Genghis Khan than can be accommodated here, but these few instances provide a glimpse of the kind of decision-maker he was. Genghis Khan was a pragmatist when it came to solving problems. He maintained the status quo in the territories he conquered but unified them with a Great Law with which they harmonized their traditions. In making decisions, Khan drew the best ideas from all parts of his great empire. To this day, his image is immortalized in the Mongolian currency in circulation, the tögrög or tugrik.

Figure 3.1 - Mongolian Money [28]

Marie Van Brittan Brown

Few have heard of Marie Van Brittan Brown, but many are quite familiar with her invention – closed circuit television and the home security camera. If this surprised you, as it did many others, chalk it up to the notion that the invention of modern electronic devices is often attributed to large corporations like Apple and Microsoft and to men. That a working-class black woman in the mid-sixties invented the remote security system and CCTV is therefore somewhat short of incredulous.

Nonetheless, it is a matter of fact. Marie Van Brittan was born on October 30, 1922, in Jamaica, Queens, New York. Very little is known of her; even her parents' names are unknown, but her mother was from Pennsylvania and her father was born in Massachusetts. It is believed that she appears to have been born into slavery but was freed at the age of 7. Her high school and college education is unknown. [29]

Marie married Albert Brown, an electronics technician. At first, she was a stay-at-home wife, but eager to do something with her life, she enrolled to become a nurse. Marie and her husband worked different shifts, and she often found herself alone at home at different hours of the night or day. It was not long before they became concerned for their safety, as they lived in a neighborhood where it would take an inordinate amount of time for law enforcement officers to arrive when called.

Marie began to work out the problem by setting up three peepholes in the door to enable access to see callers of small, average, and tall stature. She then set up a camera that could be adjusted to each of the peepholes. Not long after, Marie devised a system by which she could view the door from any room inside the house; it turned out to be a wireless television system. A radio-controlled wireless system was set up to stream video to any television in the house. This was then enhanced by attaching a two-way microphone to allow communication between the residents in the house with a caller outside. Thus far, the system only enabled a resident to know who was outside the house; it did not have any provisions in case of an emergency.

Ultimately, a feature was included that allowed someone in the house to unlock the door by remote control and allow the person outside to come in. The television, microphone, and unlocking systems worked in tandem to greatly improve home security. The system, which became known as the home surveillance device with a closed-circuit television security system, was completed when Marie turned 44 years old. This is the same system installed in homes today to keep residents safe.

Sometime thereafter, Marie invented a system that contacted emergency response personnel at the tap of a button. These innovations combined revolutionized the standard of home security and led to the systems most of us use today. And while it was initially designed for home use, Marie's invention was quickly adapted for businesses. Her invention became the foundation of CCTV surveillance systems, of which 100 million units were operating in 2016 according to a *New Scientist* report. [30]

On August 1, 1966, Marie and Albert applied for a patent entitled "Home Security System Utilizing Television Surveillance." Their application was approved on December 2, 1969, [31] under U.S. Patent Number 3,482,037. [32]For her invention, Marie Van Brittan Brown received an award from the National Science Committee. The New York Times quoted her as saying:

> A woman alone could set off an alarm immediately by pressing a button, or if the system were installed in a doctor's office, it might prevent holdups by drug addicts.[33]

— MARIE VAN BRITTAN BROWN

Even in her comments, Marie showed her pragmatism, no-nonsense approach to solving a real-world need for security in the home. She began with a problem that impacted her and her family and invested knowledge, time, and effort to resolve this problem. With the help of her electronic-technician husband, Albert, she went about it incrementally and recursively, incorporating the more recent technological advances as they came onstream. She was guided by a singular goal – to secure her family's safety in the home. The result was an innovation that responded to a need felt by everyone on the planet.

Marie lived until the age of 76. She had two children, Albert Brown Jr. and Norma Brown. Norma became, like her mother, a nurse and an inventor.

Tenzing Norgay And Edmund Hillary

> ❝ I have never regarded myself as a hero, but Tenzing undoubtedly was.[34]

— EDMUND HILLARY

> ❝ If it is a shame to be the second man on Mount Everest, then I will have to live with this shame.[35]

— TENZING NORGAY

Know that theirs were the first footsteps in the world's tallest mountain. In 1953, New Zealand explorer Edmund Hillary teamed up with 19-year-old Tibetan Sherpa Tenzing Norgay[36] to go where no man had ever gone before. But this was not science fiction. Their destination was the very real, very solid peak of Mount Everest, located 29,032 feet above where the rest of mankind trod the earth.

They may appear the odd couple, but the collaboration of Hillary and Norgay brought together the ideal combination of contemporary and traditional mountaineering experience. The Sherpa people are an indigenous group living in the valleys of the Himalayan mountains of which Everest is the highest peak. The livelihood of the Sherpas includes farming, herding, and trade. Of late, they have proven invaluable to Everest climbers because of their knowledge of logistics, terrain, and dealing with low oxygen levels. Without them, making the climb would be impossible. Their unselfish collaboration made the accomplishment possible, and their words convey their acknowledgment of this fact.

Hillary and Norgay were not the first to attempt the precipitous journey. The first attempt was in 1921, when a British expedition led by George Leigh Mallory was forced to abort by a raging storm. When asked by a journalist his reason for wanting to climb Mount Everest, Mallory answered with the now famous line, "Because it's there."

Mallory tried once more in 1922, but the failed attempt ended with the death of seven Sherpa porters in an avalanche. A third Everest expedition was launched by the British in 1924, wherein climber Edward Norton reached an elevation of 28,128 feet, only 900 vertical feet short of the summit, without the use of artificial oxygen. Four days thereafter, Mallory and Andrew Irvine made another try to reach the summit, but they were never seen alive again. In 1999, Mallory's body was discovered, largely preserved, high on Everest. He apparently fell and suffered numerous broken bones. It remains unknown whether he or Irvine ever reached the summit.[37]

These early attempts and several after them approached Everest from Tibet's Northeast Ridge route. After the second world war, Tibet was closed to all foreigners. In 1949, Nepal provided access to foreigners, and British expeditions attempted to explore the Southeast Ridge route in 1950 and 1951.

In 1952, a Swiss expedition attempted to reach the summit. Two climbers, Raymond Lambert and Tenzing Norgay, arrived at 28,210 feet, just below the South Summit, but ran short of supplies and had to turn back. Other climbs were attempted thereafter through different approaches, the closest reaching within 300 feet from the summit, but then climbers Charles Evans and Tom Bourdillon were forced to abandon their trek due to their oxygen sets malfunctioning.

Two days after Evans and Bourdillon turned back, Tenzing and Hillary set out and set their high camp at 27,900 feet. There they spent one freezing, sleepless night, then set out early the next day to reach the South Summit by 9 a.m. and a steep rocky step 40 feet high an hour later. Hillary then wedged himself in a crack in the face, now known as Hillary's step, and threw a rope down to Norgay who followed. At 11:30, the pair, at last, reached the elusive top of Mount Everest.

Since then, 6.014 people have reached the peak of Everest as of December 2021,[38] but it remains a torturous climb that has claimed more than 300 lives. The mountain's deadliest day was on April 15, 2015, when 19 people died in an avalanche at base camp following a 7.8 earthquake that killed 9,000 people and injured 23,000 in Nepal.[39]

The success of Norgay and Hillary was not theirs alone. It was the culmination of many expeditions and the mountaineers who made them beginning with Mallory in 1921. It was also the result of many lessons learned that cost lives. The weather is vicious and dynamic with temperatures reaching -38 degrees Celsius, even lower during winter. The atmospheric pressure drops to a dangerous one-third of that at sea level, causing shortness of breath, muscle pains, blurred vision, dizziness, and fatigue. Constricting blood vessels and cardiac issues have been experienced by climbers due to the drop in air pressure. The Khumbu icefall is a glacier that tends to break or burst, melting suddenly and cracking open on hot days.

There are also numerous crevasses through which unwary climbers could fall to their death. There is also the problem of traffic jams, such as seen in the picture below. Numerous hikers, sometimes numbering in the hundreds, line up along Everest's trail for hours. Being stranded along the trail can have fatal consequences particularly when the weather changes or night falls. Altitude sickness and Summit Fever can also cause unexpected and deadly reactions among climbers.[40]

Figure 3.2 - Traffic jam approaching the peak of Mount Everest[41]

These are challenges that are better known now compared to Norgay's and

Hillary's time, but they still pose tremendous risks to modern climbers. How the early explorers solved such problems as they encountered them defies the imagination. A great deal of study and preparation by the Western explorers coupled with the experience and know-how of the indigenous Sherpas are required to conquer the challenges posed by Everest. Add to this an invaluable observation:

> Good planning is important. I've also regarded a sense of humor as one of the most important things on a big expedition. When you're in a difficult or dangerous situation, or when you're depressed about the chances of success, someone who can make you laugh eases the tension.[42]

Edmund Hillary

Lessons Learned

With the benefit of hindsight, we have the privilege of gleaning what attributes are common to the protagonists in these five stories. The trait that appears to be the most important in all five cases is pragmatism. Our protagonists in these stories dealt with problems sensibly and realistically, approaching situations with a practical rather than theoretical bent.

Einstein espoused lateral thinking whereby solutions are found through observation and creativity. Curtis LeMay did what was required to accomplish his mission by learning from precedents. Genghis Khan combined the practices of many cultures but was not hesitant to discard what did not work. Marie Van Brittan Brown was prompted by the practical need to secure her home and family and worked on incremental improvements to create a device nobody else thought of. Norgay and Hillary combined their own experiences with those who had gone before them to be the first to climb to the top of the world.

In all instances, none of the problem solvers reached any ideal solution, only practical answers that produced the desired results.

Action Steps

This is an exercise in lateral thinking, or thinking outside the box as alluded to by Albert Einstein. Its purpose is to help you develop the ability to think outside conventional norms.

We begin with nine dots arranged in a square as shown below.

```
•   •   •

•   •   •

•   •   •
```

The challenge posed for you is this: Beginning at one of the dots, connect all nine by drawing four straight lines through them without lifting your pen. Try giving it a go. After you have devoted some serious effort to this problem, you could look up the solution at the end of this chapter.

Moving On

We all invariably face problems every now and then. So just as with grandma's recipes, we should not forget to look to those who have gone before for insight and counsel. In the next chapter, we will go on to discover the common misconceptions about problem-solving that we and countless others have entertained.

Key Takeaways

- Albert Einstein: "To regard old problems from a new angle requires creative imagination."
- General Curtis LeMay: "No generation ever halts to turn around and examine the vast lore acquired by their predecessors who marched along the same route; and then to adjust a future plan (or a present crisis) accordingly. Instead, they criticize the previous generations… Then they turn around and make a whole new set of mistakes all by their lonesome."
- Genghis Khan: "People conquered on different sides of the lake should be ruled on different sides of the lake."
- Marie Van Brittan Brown: "A woman alone could set off an alarm immediately by pressing a button, or if the system were installed in a doctor's office, it might prevent holdups by drug addicts."
- Edmund Hillary: "I have never regarded myself as a hero, but Tenzing undoubtedly was."

- Tenzing Norgay: "If it is a shame to be the second man on Mount Everest, then I will have to live with this shame."

Solution To The Challenge In The Action Steps

If you had tried solving the problem using conventional thinking, you would have drawn lines within the box, along its sides and diagonally across it, while trying to connect all the dots. You would have been careful not to draw outside the box because the visual arrangement of the dots suggested this constraint. But no matter how hard you tried, you would have drawn no fewer than five lines to connect all the dots if you kept your lines within the box. You would likely have drawn a figure similar to the one below.

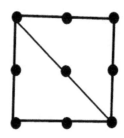

The correct solution requires you to recognize that there is no express requirement to keep your lines within the box. Therefore, you don't have to consider the box a constraint.

Look at the illustration below as your guide. Starting at the lower left corner, draw a vertical line upward but *go past the dot* at the upper left corner of the box. At the appropriate distance, draw a downward diagonal line through the middle dot at the top side of the box and the middle dot at the right side of the box. Continue the line until you reach the level of the base of the box, then draw a horizontal line leftward until you reach your starting point, the lower left corner of the box. Finally, draw one last line diagonally upward through the dot at the center of the box to the dot at the top right corner. You have connected all nine dots using four lines without lifting your pen off the surface.

It really is "thinking outside the box," isn't it?

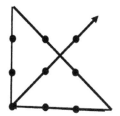

4

MISCONCEPTIONS SURROUNDING THE PROBLEM-SOLVING PROCESS

Problem-solving is "a process in which we perceive and resolve a gap between a present situation and a desired goal, with the path to the goal blocked by known or unknown obstacles." [1] This definition identifies four elements: the present situation, the desired goal, a gap that exists between them, and obstacles along the way. It is important to acknowledge these elements, because absent one of them, then a problem does not exist that requires a solution.

Let's say Farmer Joe has just gathered his harvest and is ready to sell them to customers. His farm is 20 miles away from the town market where most people go for their fresh produce. So the present situation is that the produce is at Farmer Joe's farm, and the ideal situation is that it should be in the town market. A gap exists. But does a problem exist?

If Farmer Joe has a truck that can carry his harvested yield to the market, then he simply has to load his truck and drive to town. No problem. But what if the truck doesn't have enough fuel? If a gas refilling station is close by, then he just has to gas up before his trip. No problem. But what if the truck does not want to start? If Farmer Joe knows what the problem is – say, a discharged battery or faulty starter – and he can repair it, then he only needs to conduct the repair and get the truck working. No problem.

Up to this point, the fourth element is missing: an obstacle that prevents Joe from bridging the gap.

But what if Farmer Joe just encountered this dilemma for the first time and does not know how to get the car running? The nearest mechanic also happens to be located in town, 20 miles from his farm. It's Sunday (market day) and the auto repair shop is closed. Aha! The truck's disrepair becomes an obstacle with no obvious remedy. There lies the problem.

The Five-Step Problem-Solving Strategy

The fundamental approach to problem-solving is describable in five steps. [2]

Step 1: Specify The Problem.

In class or at work, the teachers or our superiors identified and formulated for us the problems we solved. But in the real world, problems initially manifest as vague feelings that something is not right. In such instances, you have to discover the problem and formulate it into a problem statement as simply and clearly as possible. In articulating the problem, you must assess not only the problem state but also how far it differs from the goal state.

Step 2: Analyze The Problem.

Find out as much as you can about the problem. This goes beyond the superficial situation regarding what is obvious. Dig into hidden issues, different perspectives, and unforeseen impacts regarding the problem. Do research into information not readily evident, and brainstorm about likely implications.

Step 3: Formulate Possible Solutions.

As you analyze the problem, you will come to identify a wide range of solutions. This often comes in the form of brainstorming. Be creative in seeking alternatives – more is better. Pick up clues from similar problems you dealt with before, and how you resolved them.

Step 4: Evaluate Possible Solutions.

In your expansive list, you will intuitively gravitate more towards a few among them. They probably appear to you to be more viable, or you may have some knowledge regarding their practicability. Weigh the advantages and disadvantages of the possible solutions identified. Think through your options and visualize how, when, and where you may accomplish each. Consider the immediate and long-term repercussions. Map out your solutions to get a comprehensive view of your alternatives.

Step 5: Choose A Solution.

From your analysis of your choices, make a shortlist of three to five that you think are most feasible. As you near a final decision, consider three factors in making your choice. (1) Assess the compatibility of your choice with your priorities. (2) Weigh the risk of adopting this choice. Finally, (3) evaluate the workability of solution. Then, make your decision, and commit to it.

The Relationship Between Problem-Solving And Decision-Making

Decision-making is the process of identifying choices, evaluating them, and selecting the most advantageous. It has much in common with problem-solving. Talanker[3] argues in his conference paper that they are one and the same. The terms merely emphasize different aspects of the same cognitive process that is characterized by multiple stages and goal orientation.

Academic studies recommend performing the following steps to arrive at the best decision.[4] See how well they fit into the five-step problem-solving process.

- Consider the likely outcomes of each alternative. Note both the short-term and long-term repercussions.

- Compare the ease with which you can accomplish each alternative.
- Cautiously weigh the negative side effects of each alternative.
- Assess the risks involved in each choice.
- Be creative in your assessment. Do not disregard alternatives simply because you have not encountered them previously.

Apparently, the decision-making process fits in with the tail-end of the five-step problem-solving method – specifically, it is an expansion of step 5, after you have shortlisted the likely choice. Going through the decision-making stage can take a sizeable amount of time, effort, and cost; thus, it should be performed only on the most likely alternatives.

Essentialism

While engaging in high-level cognitive activities such as problem-solving, decision-making, and generally making sense of our environment, we are frequently led astray by concepts that have little relevance to the activity at hand. For example, Elmer, who is asthmatic, was told that dogs' dander triggers asthma attacks. Despite wanting to own a dog as a pet, Elmer decided against getting one because he thought all dogs cause asthma. In truth, certain dog breeds are hypoallergenic. Poodles, Maltese, and Yorkshire terriers, among many others, do not trigger allergies.

Essentialism is a belief that things possess a set of traits that makes them what they are.[5] The nature of the thing is defined by these characteristics, absent which the thing loses its essence. Lack of care in the attribution of essential traits can lead to wrong conclusions. Had Elmer realized that some dogs do not cause allergic reactions, he would have spent many happy years with a beloved canine pet. When we make decisions, we must be careful to judge on the basis of essential traits, and decide accordingly.

Essentialism has four distinct meanings. According to Phillips[6], it may mean any one of the following:

1. The attribution of certain characteristics to all members of a particular category.

2. The attribution of those characteristics to the category in ways that naturalize that which may be socially construed or created.

3. The invocation of a collectivity as either the subject or object of political action, in a way that presumes a homogeneous and unified group.

4. The policing of this collective category, the treatment of the characteristics it supposedly shares as defining characteristics that cannot be questioned or modified "without undermining an individual's claim to belong to that group."[7]

The foregoing give us the idea that it is not a simple matter to judge which traits are essential or not. Traits may be considered essential to participants being analyzed depending on the purpose for which they are being analyzed. In the case of theses and dissertations, the subjects included in the research are specifically defined in the description of the research sample. Inclusion of subjects who do not possess the essential traits for a study tends to skew the results and compromise the accuracy of the conclusion.

Myths About Problem-Solving

We all take problem-solving for granted because we engage in it every day. But there are some misconceptions about problems and solving them that we take for granted to be true. Let us examine some of them here.

Myth #1: The Word "Problem" Has An Unambiguous Meaning.

When we hear the word "problem," we automatically take it to have one clear meaning, except that it has potentially three different meanings based on scholarly literature (even more in real-world contexts). The three meanings identified by Kasser and Zhao[8] based on academic studies are:

1. A Question Proposed For Solution Or Discussion.

For example, "How can we make this world a better place?" The "problem" is actually a rhetorical question, posed for the purpose of discourse rather than arriving at a concrete answer. Problems in the guise of rhetorical propositions are not seriously in search of a practicable solution. They are merely posed for generalized discussion.

2. An Undesirable Situation, Or The Underlying Cause Of An Undesirable Situation.

For example, food shortage in general, or the post-pandemic food shortage in particular. Food shortage, in general, is an undesirable situation without a specific cause (because it may have multiple causes). The post-pandemic food shortage refers to the inadequate food supply resulting from the economic lockdown during the spread of Covid-19.

3. The Need To Map Out The Necessary Sequence Of Activities To Transform An Initial Undesirable Situation Into A Desirable Situation.

For example, "How to address the post-pandemic food shortage to ensure sufficient food supply for the general public." In this case, not only is the undesirable situation identified but also its cause. The implication is to address the cause to revert the situation from undesirable to desirable.

Myth #2: The Process Of Effective Problem-Solving Needs A Clearly Defined Problem.

There is a misconception that unless a problem is well-defined, it cannot be solved. This may be true of some situations such as academic research.

But certain real-world problems do not need to be perfectly articulated to start the solution-creation process. [9] We sometimes spend too much time identifying and segregating what we think are different problems, only to realize later on that they are parts of the same problem situation which we must also consider in finding an effective solution. Multiple related problems are information, and they direct our attention to the larger issue that responds to the root of the problems.

Early in his career as a technician at a local cable service provider, Danny received a job order from customer service to check up on a service interruption complaint by one of their subscribers. As he was preparing to leave, another call came in also complaining about service failure. After a couple of minutes, three more calls came in quick succession. Danny thought he would have his hands full responding to these complaints, but noticed that they all happened to be located in the same service area.

On a hunch that the failure experienced by these customers might be related, Danny rang up James in the engineering department. "Roger that, Danny. A container truck lost its brakes and rammed one of the posts that carried our main line. All the lines serving that area are connected to this main line, so those accounts are down for now. We'll contact customer service about this so they can inform our customers that we are on it." Danny hung up, happy that the engineering department saved him the trouble of responding to all those complaints individually.

Sometimes, we puzzle over problems that we just can't get our heads around because they lack definition. The reason we cannot define a problem with sufficient clarity is that some information is missing, but you're not sure what it is. Like Danny, we know something is wrong but need to learn more about it, as Danny learned from James. Real-world problems must be first explored and understood. The exploration process provides us with the information necessary to define the problem.

Based on this, we extend our five-step problem-solving process by two steps:

Step 1: Gather information about the current situation.

Step 2: Explore the information to determine why the situation is undesirable.

Step 3: Specify the problem.

Step 4: Analyze the problem.

Step 5: Formulate possible solutions.

Step 6: Evaluate possible solutions.

Step 7: Choose a solution.

Myth #3: There Is Always A Single Correct Solution.

When considering alternatives, we are often fixated on one correct solution when in reality, there can be several. The single solution is a myth that our school system ingrained in us. We solved well-defined problems (such as in mathematics or science) and passed the exercise with full merit only if we arrived at the "correct" answer. While this approach is ideal for learning basic principles (thus its adoption in the school system), its narrowly defined problems are sanitized versions of the real-world dilemmas that they represent.

Sam and Elise were on their dream vacation in a quaint island resort in the Pacific. One of the tourist attractions was an ancient temple set at the top of a mountain. It could be reached by climbing 1,000 winding steps carved into the mountainside by natives more than a hundred years ago. Sam, an avid historian, wanted to make the climb. Elise, however, had weak knees and opted out. "It's too difficult. I'll just wait for you here," she told Sam.

So, Sam set out, resolved to make good time so his wife would not wait too long and get bored. After the first fifteen minutes, he was panting heavily, only realizing then that the steps were too steep and the climb was proving taxing even for him. He paused three times along the way, and finally reached the top after nearly an hour.

To his surprise, he saw Elise at the top of the stairs. "What took you so long?" she said. Before he could catch his breath enough to reply, she pointed at what looked like a modern contraption behind her. "There's a lift installed a short distance from where the stairs were located. It went right to the top and was made of glass. The scene was absolutely breathtaking! The ride took 15 minutes." She smiled impishly. "And how was your trek?"

Often, we rush to judgment and take the most obvious solution. Let us not forget that there may be other answers to our problem that will likely produce the same results in simpler and more efficient ways. We just need to look for them.

Myth #4: A Single Pass Through The Problem-Solving Process Will Almost Always Provide An Optimal Solution To The Problem.

A pass-through is a single linear process from start to finish. It is an idea found in systems engineering, but it applies to many contexts. Sometimes, you have to go through a process multiple times until you find the right solution. This is called iteration, which simply means repetition.

A good example of this type of problem is hunting for your first job. Right out of school, you think that, armed with your diploma and resume, all you need to do is send in your application, take the tests given by Human Resources (HR), then show up for the interview in your best business attire. Bingo! You're employed! No, not really. If your first application gets you the job, then you would have won the jackpot – which is about one in 14 million[10], maybe even less. But you will more likely have to submit several applications for different job openings, take several tests, and appear at several interviews, before you finally get your first job.

Iteration is not for nothing, however. At every pass-through, something new is learned that is applied at the next pass-through. For each new potential employer, you learn to compose a better application letter. You improve on your resume, and you remember previous tests that you've already taken. Moreover, you learn to anticipate certain questions in the interview and come better prepared to answer them. Iterations give you the benefit of experience and added knowledge.

Myth #5: A Single Problem-Solving Approach Fits All Types Of Problems.

Many self-help problem-solving blogs attract our clicks with the promise of a one-approach-fits-all problem-solving method. Well, there isn't. Understanding that there are a wide variety of problems makes it almost intuitive for us to expect that their solutions also vary widely. Let's just take one factor, the difficulty of solving any particular problem. Ford[11] identified four categories of increasing order of difficulty for solving mathematics and science problems.

1. Easy problems can be solved in a short time with very little thought.

2. Medium problems can be solved after some thought, although they may require a few more steps to solve compared to easy problems. With some practice, they may not take too much difficulty to solve.

3. Ugly problems (as Ford called them) take a while to solve, involve much thought, take many steps, and may require using several different concepts.

4. Hard problems typically deal with one or more unknowns. Solving them requires a lot of thought and some research. It may also need some iteration (or repetition, as you may recall from our discussion on pass-throughs) through the problem-solving process as we learn more about the problem. (Iteration of the problem-solving process becomes necessary as some unknowns become known.)

The classification above applied particularly to mathematical and science problems. They may or may not apply to other problem types. It does pay to know what these categories are, though, if only to appreciate how different problems are solved.

Myth #6: All Problems Can Be Solved.

Do you know that there are literally unsolvable problems in this age, the age of computers and the Internet? The Clay Mathematics Institute (CMI) of Cambridge, Massachusetts, has designated seven mathematical problems that, it claims, cannot be solved. To put their money where their mouth is, the CMI put up a reward of a million dollars for a solution to each of the seven problems.

The problems were announced in the year 2000, and are known collectively as the Millennium Problem. The seven problems are the Riemann hypothesis, P versus NP problem, Birch and Swinnerton-Dyer conjecture, Hodge conjecture, Navier-Stokes equation, Yang-Mills theory, and Poincaré conjecture. In 2006, Grigori Perelman, a Russian mathematician, published a solution for the Poincaré conjecture although he refused the reward offered by the CMI in 2010.[12] To date, nobody has solved the remaining six problems.

The existence of the Millennium Problem suggests that there are problems that apparently cannot be solved. Or maybe, like the Poincaré conjecture, a solution is somewhere out there but it will take an indefinite duration and much effort before someone provides a solution. Twenty-two years have passed; for all intents and purposes, we can declare that in this lifetime, at least, the Millennium Problem cannot be solved.

How about non-mathematical problems? Well, there are static problematic situations and dynamic problematic situations. Static conditions are stable and changes do not happen, nor are expected to happen. Dynamic conditions are characterized by changing situations that impact the creation of the problem and its surrounding specifics.[13] But some problems are static in the short term, then become dynamic in the long term.

In the 14th century, the bubonic plague killed 25 million, nearly one-third of Europe's population. In 1860, another outbreak that started in China and spread to North America killed about 10 million people. During those times, people afflicted with the disease had practically no chance of survival; it was a problem without a solution. Today, the bacteria that caused the plague is still present, but with rapid diagnosis, antibiotic treatment, good sanitation, and pest control, the disease has little probability of escalating into a pandemic.[14] Scientific discoveries, technological developments, and cultural modernization have turned a static problem into a dynamic one that is capable of a solution.

Problems can be remedied without being solved. According to Kasser and Zhao[15], there are four ways they are remedied:

1. *Solving the problem.* This happens when a decision-maker selects the optimal solution – the best possible alternative. Mathematical problems are

always in search of the optimal solution, although it may not always be possible.

2. Resolving the problem. Here, the decision-maker does not arrive at the best absolute choice despite his best efforts, but achieves a result that is good enough or acceptable. Management or household problems fall in this category because of their immediate constraints and the need for a practical solution (even if it may not be perfect) to sufficiently address the need.

3. Dissolving the problem. The decision-maker dissolves a problem when he reformulates it to produce an outcome in which the original problem no longer has any significance. These refer to the innovative solutions. The morning rush traffic may be hopeless in terms of accommodating all the cars on the road. However, enabling several people to work from home is an innovation that can dissolve the traffic problem.

4. Absolving the problem. This situation occurs when a decision-maker ignores a problem in the hope that it will disappear on its own. The decision-maker may intentionally ignore a problem when the cost of seeking a remedy is too much, or when the technology required to solve it is unavailable, unknown, or unaffordable. It may also include broad problems where some stakeholders have an interest in not seeking a solution. In most countries, voter integrity is assured by requiring voter identification, thus solving the problem of election fraud. In some areas of the U.S., voter identification (I.D.) is rejected as a matter of policy, thereby propagating or absolving the problem.

Action Steps

This is an exercise in distinguishing among solution, resolution, dissolution, and absolution. Could you identify the category to which each scenario belongs?

Jack and his mother lived in poverty. Jack's mother sent her son to sell their cow in the market.

Scenario 1: Jack sold the cow for five magic beans. His mother threw the beans on the ground, and they grew into giant beanstalks. Jack climbed the beanstalk and returned with a goose that laid golden eggs.

Scenario 2: Jack sold the cow for a modest sum of money and brought the proceeds home to his mother.

Scenario 3: Jack told his mother to keep the cow, and he went out to find work that paid a steady wage.

Scenario 4: Jack told his mother to keep the cow. Instead, they applied for welfare from the government.

You may check your answers against the key found at the end of this chapter.

Moving On

Problem-solving methods cover a wide range of approaches. Debunked myths should not prevent us from finding the best course of action to take. The following chapter describes the concrete steps we can take to solve any problem we may face.

Key Takeaways

- The five-step problem-solving strategy is the most fundamental approach to solving problems.
- Decision-making comprises the final steps of the problem-solving process.
- It is a myth that correct problem-solving requires a clearly-defined problem or that there is always a single solution.
- Solving a problem may require several pass-throughs before finding an optimal solution.
- There is no single approach that solves all types of dilemmas.

Key To The Exercise In The Action Steps

Before you can categorize the scenarios, you first have to identify the problem. If you said that Jack's problem was how he could sell the cow, then your answers would be misguided. The problem is suggested in the first statement: Jack and his mother lived in poverty. The reason she was asking him to sell the cow was to alleviate the effects of their poverty. Knowing this, then the following are how the scenarios should be categorized.

Solution: Scenario 3

By getting a job that pays a steady (and presumably sufficient) wage, Jack solves their situation in a sustainable way. He has eliminated the root cause of their problem, which is their poverty.

Resolution: Scenario 2

Jack does exactly as his mother tells him to, which would alleviate their situation only for a short while until the proceeds of the sale are used up. If you identified the problem as "How Jack should go about selling the cow," then this would have been the solution. But as you see, the real problem they wished to solve, their poverty, remains. Thus, this is an acceptable, but not absolute, solution.

Dissolution: Scenario 1

This is, of course, the fairy tale plot. But Jack did not solve the problem. He and his mother became the beneficiaries of fortuitous events that rendered their original problem (their poverty) insignificant. Much like winning the lotto, good luck intervenes and suddenly, the winner's financial worries become irrelevant.

Absolution: Scenario 4

Jack and his mother may apply for welfare to alleviate their poverty, but this does not solve the problem. Government welfare is meant to be a temporary bridge between periods of gainful employment. By relying on welfare as a permanent source of subsistence, Jack and his mother are ignoring the problem of their poverty, possibly because they have an interest in not seeking a solution.

5

MAIN APPROACHES TO PROBLEM-SOLVING, THEIR STRATEGIES AND TOOLS

T he king was facing a serious problem that could spell life or death for his countrymen. Should he engage the advancing invaders to prevent them from reaching Sparta? Or should he and his people submit to Persian domination? The legendary king visited the Ephors to consult the magistrates on the prospects for war. The elders consulted the Oracle, who was the most beautiful teenage girl in Sparta. In a drug-induced trance, the Oracle decreed that Sparta must not go to war during the

Greek festival of the Carneia. The decision was final; the problem was solved.

Of course, all of us who watched the movie *300*[1] or remember Greek history know the rest of the story. King Leonidas I was forced to take a small contingent of soldiers and eventually lost the Battle of Thermopylae. Artistic license notwithstanding, any reasonable person today would regard this depiction with a large grain of salt. What rational monarch would give credence to "a drunken adolescent girl" (the king's words) on the matter of national security and defense? Does this decision-making process make sense?

But even in this age of space travel and the Internet, we still retain some vestiges of the mystical "Oracle" when making decisions. You must have heard of Paul the Octopus in Germany, who accurately predicted the winners of several international sports events. Paul correctly guessed Spain's victory over the home team in the 2010 World Cup, attracting the ire of German soccer fans who threatened to eat him.

Another famous mystic beast is Eli the Orangutan of Salt Lake City, who correctly picked the winners of seven consecutive NFL championships. Two politically literate tigers and a brown bear in Russia correctly chose Joseph Biden to win over Donald Trump, ironically. But probably the most popular animal oracle is Punxsutawney Phil, a woodchuck renowned for forecasting the end of winter and the beginning of spring.[2] People rely on these animals to help them decide whether to place a sporting bet or prepare for the spring planting season.

For more discerning decision-makers, there are at least five approaches to solving problems, none of which involve animals. These are the rational, collaborative, creative, historical, and organic approaches. Why so many methods? It is because problems are numerous and diverse. So, therefore, are the strategies and tools to solve them.

The following are only a few of these methods, which we will briefly describe. Our purpose here is to give you a small sampling of the broad spectrum of alternatives available at problem solvers' fingertips. Thus, we will define each approach and tool only enough to provide an idea and appreciation of its use.

Rational

By and large, the rational approach is the most frequently adopted problem-solving method because it works for a wide range of problems. From its name, it employs reasoning as the basis of its decision-making process. In many academic studies, the rational model of decision-making (aka problem-solving) is characterized by the use of "facts and information, analysis, and a step-by-step procedure"[3] to solve a problem. All methods of problem-solving use these elements to some extent, but the rational method relies on them almost entirely in a systematic and organized manner.

The Scientific Method

The method that best exemplifies the rational approach is the scientific method. There are five steps in the scientific method: state the problem, form the hypothesis, observe and experiment, interpret data, and draw conclusions.[4] It parallels the five-step problem-solving procedure we described at the beginning of this chapter. Everyone who has taken elementary and high school science subjects is familiar with this approach.

Hypothesis Testing

Hypothesis testing is essentially the heart of the scientific method, although it is more commonly associated with statistical tests of numerical data. Generally speaking, a hypothesis is a theory to be tested. It is a scientific guess in search of proof. In the statistical field, it is defined as "a tentative assertion of a formal statement of theory (testable or refutable) that shows how two or more variables are expected to relate to one another."[5] Such tests include correlation, regression, significant difference, and the like. A null hypothesis is tested and accepted or rejected depending on how the test result compares to the significance level.

Pro-Con-Fix

The pro-con-fix process is a simple tool for decision-making. It is an extension of the pros and cons list decision-making tool, so we will first acquaint ourselves with the latter.[6] The pros-and-cons method involves listing the potential positive and negative outcomes of a decision. Begin by formatting a chart with two columns which you fill with brainstormed advantages in one column and the disadvantages in the other. You could expand this by writing another set of advantages and disadvantages from the perspective of the third person – the impacts of the option on others. Then, for each disadvantage, think and write down about ways you can adopt to fix it. This is the "fix" in the pro-con-fix. This method of problem-solving best addresses a situation where you would want to compare two mutually exclusive choices with each other – so-called binary decisions. Problems answerable by "Yes" or "No" are one type of binary situation ideal for this method.

The Simplex Process

The simplex process is a mathematical tool used to solve a particular type of problem, namely linear programming. The word "simplex" is a mathematical term referring to a set of points in a geometric region that corresponds to an optimal solution to a linear programming problem. Put simply, it is a solution arrived at graphically. "Linear programming" is frequently applied to management problems involving the allocation of scarce resources among a group of activities or projects. Linear programming may be used to apportion raw materials, distribute personnel, or allocate funding among concurrent projects to minimize costs and maximize outcomes.[7]

<u>Sorting, Chronologies, And Timelines</u>

These methods are ways of organizing and making sense of data. We are familiar with these procedures because we have been using them since grade school. Sorting is arranging a list of options systematically according to some criterion (or criteria) such as type, class, ease of execution, cost, etc. Chronologies are the arrangement of events according to their occurrence in time. The chronology of a production process first lists the ordering and delivery of raw materials, followed by steps in the assembly line process, and ending with packaging and delivery of the finished goods. Timelines are chronologies that are extended to include tabular or linear graphic representations of sequences of events.

Collaborative

Collaborative problem-solving involves multiple people working together to solve a problem. Members of the group collaborate typically by brainstorming or a similar process by which they provide their opinions and suggestions to reach a solution. The participants should therefore be diverse individuals who are impacted by the problem situation and its proposed changes. After implementing the change, the participants should provide continuous feedback to ensure that the change solves the problem.

Stakeholder Analysis

Stakeholders are independent parties who are affected or involved in a problem situation, and therefore are interested in its solution. Stakeholder analysis is the process of identifying and evaluating stakeholders from the perspective of an organization.[8] The action precipitating the change is, therefore, one taken by an institution, a corporation, or similar large establishments that may potentially harm people when it acts in its own interests. The decision-making process in stakeholder analysis does not necessarily involve active participation by stakeholder representatives in the discussion, particularly in organizational decision-making. However, some procedures, such as surveys or interviews, should elicit first-hand information from them to validate the analysis. To prevent potential harm, stakeholders should have a voice in crafting decisions that affect them.

Devil's Advocacy

One procedure aimed at facilitating problem-solving is the devil's advocacy technique. This technique was developed in the late 1960s to aid complex problem-solving and corporate strategic decision-making. When a group has identified a recommended decision, plan, or action, it is then subjected to a critique by another group or a designated expert. The critique aims to raise questions about the plan, its underlying assumptions, and possible weaknesses. Based on the critique, the plan is revised and the revision is again critiqued. This back-and-forth process is repeated until all are satisfied that the questions have been adequately addressed. The devil's advocacy technique is useful in preventing groupthink. It is built on the premise that conflict is constructive for problem-solving.[9]

Creative

The creative approach parallels the rational approach but places a greater emphasis on creativity, or "novel associations that are useful."[10] Solvers who use this approach dwell more on ideation techniques, which are activities aimed at generating new ideas. The following are some ideation techniques.

Brainstorming

Brainstorming is a method of generating spontaneous ideas in a free-wheeling environment where criticism is ruled out. Maximizing the quantity, rather than the quality, of ideas is the goal of a brainstorming session. While criticism is not acceptable, the combination and improvement of earlier ideas are welcome.[11]Brainstorming may be done by a group or an individual.

Abstraction

Abstraction is the process of eliminating or filtering out the characteristics of problems that are not essential to concentrate on those that are essential. Specific details and patterns that do not form part of the general idea of the problem are ignored. Abstraction also means the mapping of a problem onto a generalized representation.[12] The general representation that emerges is known as the model.[13] Abstracting and decomposing a problem to its bare elements helps simplify the problem before it is solved.

Divergent Or Lateral Thinking

Divergent or lateral thinking is the process of generating unique or new ideas in solving a problem. We often refer to it as "thinking outside the box." It refers to spontaneous, free-flowing thinking that explores solutions frequently overlooked by mainstream and traditional thinkers.

Individuals with uncommon insight and creativity are good lateral thinkers.[14]

Means-End Analysis

The means-end analysis is a problem-solving technique that involves "the deliberate planning and execution of a chain of actions to achieve a goal, and occurs in situations where an obstacle ... preventing the achievement of a goal must initially be removed."[15] This technique makes it easier to control the entire process of problem-solving because it begins with a predetermined goal. Actions are then chosen that lead to that goal. Both forward and backward researches are conducted with the end goal in mind.[16]

Problem Restatement

In any problem-solving situation, but more especially in academic studies, the formulation of a good problem statement is crucial. For theses and dissertations, the problem statement must (1) be clear and precise, devoid of sweeping generalizations, (2) identify the subject of study specifically, (3) state an overarching question and the key factors or variables, (4) specify the key concepts, boundaries or parameters while maintaining some generalizability, (5) avoid jargon, and (6) yield inferences and not mere descriptive data.[17] While this strict definition pertains to academic research, it illustrates how properly stating a problem guides its solution.

Most problems benefit from the statement-restatement (also known as problem-restatement) technique developed by Osborn and Parnes. It involves digging deeper to find the root of the problem and consequently reframing it. The problem evolves so that you gain a fresh perspective that generates creative and valuable solutions while focusing on the core of the problem.[18] The problem-restatement technique is the fourth step of a six-step creative problem-solving procedure developed by Alex Osborn and Sidney J. Parnes.[19]

Historical

Reinventing the wheel is futile; it is time-consuming, inefficient, and entirely unnecessary. This is the wisdom behind the historical approach. When you face a problem that has precedent, revising the past solution is worthwhile and prudent. The work of others who have solved the same problem in the past may guide you to develop a solution to your current problem. The following techniques make use of previous knowledge and experience as the key to problem-solving.

Algorithm

An algorithm is an exact list of instructions that performs a computation or solves a problem. The procedure lists the actions step by step much as a machine (hardware or software) would conduct the process. Algorithms frequently refer to mathematical instructions executed by computers to solve recurrent or iterative problems; thus, they are typically used in applications involving artificial intelligence.[20] Algorithms, by their nature, are solutions to problems already solved in the past, for which reason they are classified as historical.

One example is the divide-and-conquer algorithm. It is a strategy for solving large problems by (1) breaking the problem into smaller sub-problems, (2) solving the sub-problems, and (3) combining them to get the desired result.[21] Breaking down the larger problem is not only done once but recursively (repeatedly) until the sub-problems are small enough to solve.

Analogy

Analogical problem-solving or reasoning involves comparison, applying prior knowledge to a current situation.[22] Analogy relies on a broader perspective than a simple algorithmic approach to solving current problems by using cognitive psychology to draw parallels with past problematic situations. A past solution must not be a constraint on a present problem to the extent of stifling creativity. Thus, when may an analogy be made between a past and present situation?

When drawing an analogy, expert decision-makers tend to rely on superficial similarity rather than a more in-depth structural similarity between the historical model and the present problem. They also look for a regularity between the problem domain and the likely solution domain of the historical and current situation.[23] The premises for drawing an analogy are, therefore, a combination of general and specific similarities between the historical and present cases.

Heuristics

Mental shortcuts that ease the cognitive load of making a decision are called heuristics. Their main advantage is expediency, but they cannot guarantee whether the method is optimal or rational. They are formed based on previous experiences concerning similar problems, which is why we categorize heuristics as historical. When information is lacking and time is scarce, we may often rely on heuristics to make a quick and necessary judgment. There are many instances when we decide quickly that we may call heuristics. Acting on "gut feel" or "intuition" are part of heuristics.

Herbert Simon, who introduced the concept of heuristics in the 1950s, suggested that human judgment is subject to cognitive limitations. We do not always have the luxury of weighing all the pros and cons of the various alternatives in making rational decisions. There is always the danger of giving way to cognitive biases and stereotypes in making rushed decisions.[24] But with certain precautions, heuristics may be a useful tool in making hurried but necessary decisions.

Trial And Error

One of the heuristic methods we frequently resort to is trial and error, also known as "guess-and-check" or "hit-and-miss"[25]. This process involves repeated and diverse attempts at finding a solution until success is achieved or the solver stops trying. Seldom does trial-and-error produce satisfactory results on the first try, so it should be used only when you can make multiple attempts at little or no risk.

Trial-and-error is not advisable when the cost of making mistakes is high, the consequences of a mistake may be serious, and you might compromise your reputation by the misses you are likely to make. If the problem solver is inexperienced, then this method will require multiple loops and intensive thinking processes focused on learning about the problem and its solution options.[26]

Rule Of Thumb

The rule of thumb is "a broadly accurate guide or principle, based on experience or practice rather than theory."[27] It is difficult to describe what rules of thumb are or how they are developed. Rules of thumb are informal pieces of practical advice[28], which means that there is no official authority that endorses or validates them. It is built on experiences that some people may find relevant, but not others. Further, they are simplified generalizations of someone's experience; thus, they may ignore more complex but important facets of the problem situation. Finally, they are not based on science or theory, and, therefore, cannot be systematically corroborated. Rules of thumb cannot, therefore, be deemed entirely accurate. Nevertheless, the frequent use of some rule-of-thumb practices by a homogeneous group of people (e.g., science students) tends to have a positive effect on the group's conceptual understanding of the rule as a convention.[29] For simple decisions to simple problems, it is better to rely on rules of thumb rather than having no benchmarks to rely on at all.

Educated Guess

An educated guess is simply what its name implies. It is no more than a guess, although it is made using judgment supported by some knowledge and experience. In academic research, an educated guess refers to a hypothesis, a declaration based on experience that needs to be confirmed by more rigorous proof or evidence.[30] Reliance on an educated guess, therefore, depends largely on the expertise of the person making the guess and the degree to which the guess conforms to past knowledge. The more astute the person guessing and the more consistent the guess is with established theory, the more likely the guess will be correct.

Weighted Ranking

The weighted ranking or weighted score technique is a mathematical method of evaluating several choices based on a set of decision criteria. The procedure for this is straightforward. First, enumerate the criteria for judging the alternatives. These should consist of qualities that the ideal decision should possess. Thereafter, assign numerical weights to each criterion depending on its importance in solving the problem. The weights are expressed in terms of percentage points or decimal ratios, all adding up to 100% or 1.00 respectively. The assignment of weights is based on your past understanding of similar problems; thus, it is generally subjective and grounded on historical experience.

After the weights have been apportioned, rate each alternative according to each criterion listed. The scores can range from 1 to 5 or 1 to 10 in ascending order. If the range were higher, the separation among the scores would be wider for better results. Multiply the scores by their assigned weights, then total the results to obtain the weighted average. The alternative with the highest weighted average will correspond to the best possible decision.

Probability/Decision Tree, Matrices

There are a host of other mathematical methods that variably make use of historical data to find a solution to problems. Probability and decision trees are tools in general mathematics and statistics used to solve problems in engineering, business, economics, and similar fields. Check out the following tree diagram that calculated the chances of passengers surviving the sinking of the Titanic.

Figure 5.1 – Decision Tree 31

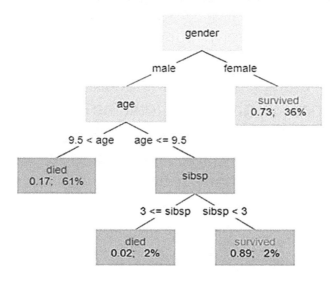

Survival of passengers on the Titanic

Matrices (singular matrix) are also decision-supporting tools wherein the data are presented in a rectangular array – a table where numbers or elements are arranged in rows and columns. The following figure is that of a four-quadrant matrix.

Figure 5.2 - Decision-making habits matrix [32]

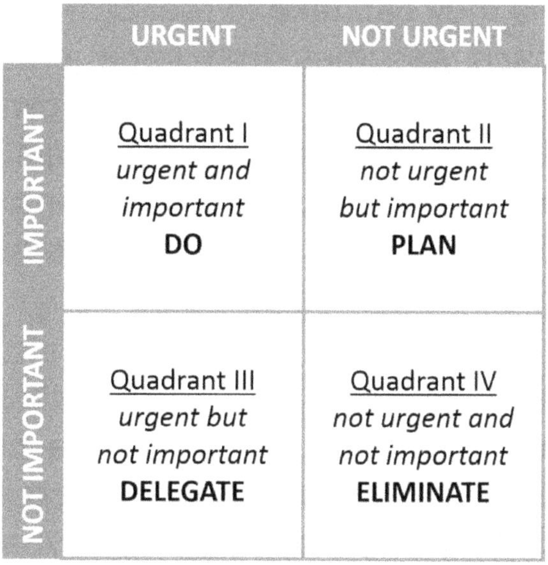

	URGENT	**NOT URGENT**
IMPORTANT	Quadrant I *urgent and* *important* **DO**	Quadrant II *not urgent* *but important* **PLAN**
NOT IMPORTANT	Quadrant III *urgent but* *not important* **DELEGATE**	Quadrant IV *not urgent and* *not important* **ELIMINATE**

The visual presentation of the data and choices in decision trees and matrices greatly facilitates the decision-making process by juxtaposing elements relative to each other.

Organic

The organic approach to problem-solving calls for the solvers to identify their mission, vision, and values, and the actions they can take to realize them. The approach assumes that large problems cannot merely be fixed by following a linear sequence of generic steps. The problem-solving process must conform to the nature of the decision-makers. The organic approach is frequently[33]encountered in the strategic planning processes of organizations. It takes into account the corporate culture of the organization and may account for stakeholder-organization dynamics, quality-of-life considerations, and social-ethical-moral standards. For instance, the selection of a company's suppliers considers not only costs and product quality, but also the ethical compliance of their operations − i.e., choice of sustainable raw materials, carbon footprint minimization, and prevention of child labor practices.

Action Steps

The following story describes five situations that describe how different problems about planning a wedding were addressed. For each of the five elements, identify which type of problem-solving strategy was used. You have five choices: Rational, Creative, Collaborative, Historical, and Organic. There are five problem-solving situations and five strategies. Some of the situations may be associated with multiple strategies and vice-versa. But there is only one best match for each.

After you have made your matches, compare your answers with those at the end of the chapter.

Monica is getting married next year. Like most excited brides-to-be, she wanted to get planning right away. Those who have gone through the rituals of planning a wedding, there are a hundred and one issues that need to be attended to.

1. The WEDDING VENUE. When and where should they set the wedding? Monica always wanted to get married in the church where her parents were wed, at the La Catedral de Nuestra Señora del Perpetuo Socorro. Her family's custom is to set the ceremony at sunrise, to signify beginnings (evenings signify endings). It should be at a full moon to bless the union with blissfulness and romance. Yanni, the prospective groom, has happily agreed to these arrangements, consistent with tradition.

2. The RECEPTION. Since Monica is keen on financial matters, she had a target budget in mind. Then she and Yanni planned to canvass the restaurants within a two-mile radius of the church. They will first inquire whether the place will be available on the date of the wedding. They will then visit each available site and ask for their menu and prices. The couple will then shortlist the likely choices, and rank them according to their preference. They will set a tentative booking for their top choices,

pending the results of the wedding tasting.

3. The BRIDAL GOWN. Monica is a graduate of fine arts and had some unique ideas about the gown she wanted to wear. Her mother and sisters had many suggestions, but here Monica drew the line. "I will design my own gown!" she said. She then did some solo brainstorming about how she can combine traditional and avant-garde features, using tulle, satin, lace, and mother-of-pearl beads to create the gown of her dreams. She also designed the gowns of her entourage, including the maid-of-honor, bridesmaids, and flower girls.

4. The ENTERTAINMENT. Because she already had so much to attend to, Monica asked her maid of honor and bridesmaids to create the program during the reception. They excitedly set a brainstorming session for all the activities they will include in the program, including speeches, games, and musical numbers. They will also get to decide.

5. Finally, the HONEYMOON location and itinerary Based on their artistic inclinations and the feedback of friends and colleagues, Monica and Yanni will honeymoon in Italy. They will spend most of their time in Florence, the "little city, tucked amid the Tuscan hills, [that] casts a long shadow through history," according to the online travel guide.[34] The couple will visit the wellspring of the Renaissance, home of the famous Medici family, and the place that inspired Michelangelo's *David* and Brunelleschi's *Duomo*. Their itinerary lists the various Italian museums, art galleries, vineyards, and historical sites in a guided tour.

Moving On

King Leonidas was right to rely on reason and judgment rather than the proclamations of an oracle. Nevertheless, he showed wisdom and statesmanship in deferring to tradition when executing his decision. As leaders, we should cling to the strength of our convictions, particularly in the most pernicious circumstances. Whatever approach we choose, our problem-solving will be better grounded if combined with the tools described in the next chapter.

Key Takeaways

- The various approaches to problem-solving include rational, collaborative, creative, historical, and organic methods.
- The rational approach is systematic and informed by facts and logic.
- The collaborative approach involves multiple people pooling their efforts to solve a problem.
- The creative approach places a greater emphasis on useful, novel associations.
- The historical approach seeks guidance from solutions developed by others in the past.

- The organic approach involves solutions that embody considerations involving values, culture, quality of life, and social-ethical-moral standards.

Answers To The Challenge In The Action Steps

1. Wedding venue – Organic. The decisions made conformed with the customs and cultural values of Monica's social background and heritage.

2. Reception – Rational. The choices of the couple were made along practical and logical considerations.

3. Bridal gown – Creative. The design was the result of the bride's distinctive taste and artistry.

4. Entertainment – Collaborative. The decisions resulted from the collegial efforts of a group.

5. Honeymoon – Historical. The choice of destination and activities by the couple relied on the past experiences of others and a guided tour prepared by a travel agent.

6

THE COST-BENEFIT ANALYSIS OF SOLVING PROBLEMS

This is an interesting anecdote suggested by Liz Jin[1] that underscores the cost of problem-solving. A company produced widgets in several factories across the country and several other international branches. At the end of the assembly lines, the finished widgets were packaged in cardboard boxes that were loaded into pallets and shipped off to wholesale customers and retail outlets.

One day, the company received a stinging complaint from a long-time customer who typically bought in bulk. During the last delivery, several of the boxes off-loaded from the pallet were empty. The valued customer called the CEO directly to lodge his complaint and demanded immediate replacements at the company's expense.

The CEO immediately sent a memo informing the factories of this incident, and issued a stern warning that a repeat of this incident would not be tolerated. He also ordered the quality control (QC) department to study the incident and arrive at a solution posthaste to systematically prevent any future recurrence.

The quality control group immediately convened a special task force that hired numerous consultants and specialists to re-engineer the assembly line process. After months of production floor walk-throughs and interviews and a week of intense meetings, QC finally submitted their recommended working plan to the

CEO that called for re-designing the box, re-aligning the assembly line, establishing the position of Box Manager who would head a team of box inspectors prior to shipment, and retraining factory workers to comply with a new 12-point quality control checklist. The estimated price tag for the proposal ran into tens of thousands of dollars. This did not include the fees already paid to the experts and consultants.

Hesitant to greenlight the sizeable investment, an item in the QC report caught the CEO's interest. One factory reported a perfect track record of having no empty boxes. He decided to visit this outperformer. As he inspected the assembly line, the CEO noticed an electric fan strategically positioned facing the assembly line at the point the filled boxes were conveyed to the pallets. He summoned the general manager and inquired about the fan. The manager replied, "One of the workers came up with this idea. When they were informed of the issue about the empty boxes, the assembly line worker went to the hardware store and bought the fan."

The heavy-duty industrial electric stand fan was strong enough to knock off the light empty boxes as they came down the conveyor belt. Therefore, only boxes that were filled with widgets made it onto the pallet. The cost of one heavy-duty industrial electric fan: $79.95.

The Importance Of Cost-Benefit Analysis In Problem-Solving

The CEO in this amusing anecdote should have promoted the assembly worker on the spot and dismissed the QC department staff. The QC staff were overly focused on finding a highly technical solution to the problem that they forgot to explore more rudimentary answers. Moreover, their recommendation would have inflated their operating expenses unnecessarily. The story underscores the need for a cost-benefit analysis before a decision is made.

A cost-benefit analysis (CBA) is a process of measuring the net benefits of a decision – that is, the value of the benefits derived minus the cost incurred in taking such action. Projecting the likely benefits and costs of undertaking a course of action is a prudent and important step before committing to a decision. It is vital for business decisions that involve large sums of money, but also for personal decisions to conserve our limited financial resources. The bottom line is that if the desired goal may be achieved by an alternative that maximizes benefits and minimizes costs, that alternative is the wiser choice.

Steps In Cost-Benefit Analysis

There are several types of cost-benefit analyses, each with a different procedure. You may have heard of the benefit-cost ratio, the incremental cost-benefit ratio, and the payback period, among others.

The method we will focus on is the net present value method, which is one of the more popular techniques for comparing alternatives because of its practical concepts.

Step 1: Specify the set of alternatives to be compared, and from whose perspective the costs and benefits are to be assessed.

Step 2: List the tangible costs and benefits of undertaking the proposed solution. Determine their value based on market prices.

Step 3: List intangible costs and benefits. Estimate the hypothetical value of these intangibles according to commonly used valuation techniques.

Step 4: If the costs and benefits stretch over several periods, derive their present value.

Step 5: Weigh the importance of each cost or benefit depending on their importance to the decision being made.

Step 6: Add up all the weighted present values of the costs and the benefits, and derive the net benefit (that is, subtract the total costs from the total benefits).

Step 7: Formulate a conclusion.

We will illustrate this process with a hypothetical problem later in this chapter. But first, let's clarify.

Why Minimize The Number Of Alternatives

The first step in finding a solution is to narrow your alternatives. Why? Because you would naturally want to conserve your time, effort, attention, and resources while still arriving at the best solution. Much like a beauty pageant with scores of beautiful candidates, judges must narrow their choices to the "finalists," maybe five or even three, before they commence the in-depth assessment of the most likely candidates.

Types Of Costs And Benefits

The next step is to identify the costs and the benefits. There are two types of costs and benefits, tangible and intangible. Let's get a better understanding of their meaning.

Identifying and valuing tangible costs and benefits is much easier than identifying and valuing intangible costs and benefits. Tangibles are readily quantifiable. They can be connected to a material expense or income, or a measurable increase or decrease in monetary value. On the other hand, intangible costs and benefits are more difficult to identify and value because they are not material and therefore valuing them is subjective. Some people think that intangibles are imaginary or not real. This cannot be further from the truth. Intangibles are real, and intangible costs and benefits have palpable impacts on our lives and situations.

The following are examples of tangible and intangible costs and benefits for households and businesses.

Households	
Tangible costs	**Tangible benefits**
Energy, lights, heating	Rent savings (if owned)
Water	Energy savings (if solar-panel
Telephone and Internet services	powered)
Professional house cleaning	Water savings (rainwater
services	harvesting)
Plumbing	Rental income (sub-let)
Rent payments	Home equity appreciation (home
Food and groceries	ownership)
Family transportation	
Home repair	
Real property tax	
Intangible costs	**Intangible benefits**
House wear and	Peace of mind (home ownership)
tear/obsolescence	Security and privacy
Car depreciation	Family well-being
Housewife's/husband's forgone	Community fraternity
employment	

Businesses	
Tangible costs	Tangible benefits
Employees' salaries and wages	Profits
Raw materials	Tax credits, shields
Utility expenses	Asset building
Other operating expenses	Shareholder wealth building
Capital expenditures	Income distribution
Intangible costs	Intangible benefits
Negative brand perception	Goodwill
Environment degradation	Positive brand perception
Land, air, and water pollution	Brand loyalty
Resource erosion	Providing livelihood to employees
Opportunity costs	Promoting supply chain productivity
	Social goods and services
	Promoting the standard of living

Computing Values Over Time

For those who are not too keen on mathematics, this section may somewhat overwhelm you but kindly bear with us. The computational aspect is not so important in terms of numbers and calculations as is the principle behind them. This principle is the time value of money.

When weighing the costs and benefits you will likely incur, you must realize that cash flows that happen closer to the present are more valuable than cash flows that occur further into the future.

The time value of money has its roots in compounding interest, which is the cornerstone principle behind all banking and business transactions. Compound interest is simply interest earned on interest. Let's briefly illustrate this.

Supposing your grandfather gave you $100 for your 15th birthday. (Grandparents are usually more generous than parents.) Instead of spending this on a computer game module, you use it to open a bank prime savings account at 10% interest. You then forget about it until your 25th birthday when you decide to look up how much your account contains. You will be surprised because over the 10 years you left your money in the bank, this is what happened.

A	B	C	D	E
	Begin Bal.	Int. rate	Interest	End Bal.
Birthday	E of year before	10%	B X C	B + D
15th	-	-	-	100.00
16th	100.00	0.10	10.00	110.00
17th	110.00	0.10	11.00	121.00
18th	121.00	0.10	12.10	133.10
19th	133.10	0.10	13.31	146.41
20th	146.41	0.10	14.64	161.05
21st	161.05	0.10	16.11	177.16
22nd	177.16	0.10	17.72	194.87
23rd	194.87	0.10	19.49	214.36
24th	214.36	0.10	21.44	235.79
25th	235.79	0.10	23.58	**259.37**

Let's go through the table. You deposit $100 when you were 15 and it starts to earn interest over the following year. When you turned 16, one year after, your account earned 10% interest or $10, so your money in the bank is $100 plus $10 or $110.

The fun thing about compounding is that the entire ending balance becomes your new principal, or the interest-earning amount. Over your 16th year, you don't just earn $10 interest, but $11. Your new principal then becomes $121. This goes on for 10 years until you turn 25 when your account amounts to $259.37. The value of your $100 compounded for 10 years at 10% is the princely sum of $259.37, more than double the original amount. The additional $159.37 is the time value of your money.

Now, how does the value of money over time impact your assessment of costs and benefits? By now, you must have realized that the decisions you make today will have both positive and negative repercussions in the future that may be tangible or intangible.

Present Value Computations

In the birthday-gift exercise, we made our decision by computing the value of your birthday gift in the future – that is, on your 25th birthday. But not all costs and benefits could be compared based on their future values because they may mature at different times – 10, 20, or 5 years from now, for instance. We need a single point in time at which to compare costs and benefits that occur at different times. The best and most common practice is to derive their *present values* because there is only one point in time that can be designated as the present.

In the example wherein you received a single sum of $100 from your grandfather at present and you saved it at a compounding rate of 10% for ten years, you derived a *future value* of $259.37. If the problem were reversed and you needed $259.37 ten years in the future at a rate of 10%, how much should you deposit now to reach that? Simple – by multiplying the future value of $259.37 by its *present value factor.* You can find it in a table such as the one below.

Figure 6.1 - Present value factor table of a single sum [2]

n	1%	2%	3%	4%	5%	6%	8%	10%
1	0.9901	0.9804	0.9709	0.9615	0.9524	0.9434	0.9259	0.9091
2	0.9803	0.9612	0.9426	0.9246	0.9070	0.8900	0.8573	0.8265
3	0.9706	0.9423	0.9151	0.8890	0.8638	0.8396	0.7938	0.7513
4	0.9610	0.9239	0.8885	0.8548	0.8227	0.7921	0.7350	0.6830
5	0.9515	0.9057	0.8626	0.8219	0.7835	0.7473	0.6806	0.6209
6	0.9421	0.8880	0.8375	0.7903	0.7462	0.7050	0.6302	0.5645
7	0.9327	0.8706	0.8131	0.7599	0.7107	0.6651	0.5835	0.5132
8	0.9235	0.8535	0.7894	0.7307	0.6768	0.6274	0.5403	0.4665
9	0.9143	0.8368	0.7664	0.7026	0.6446	0.5919	0.5003	0.4241
10	0.9053	0.8204	0.7441	0.6756	0.6139	0.5584	0.4632	0.3855

You could find an expanded table of this in almost any financial textbook or reference book, or on the Internet.[3] It is a standard table that provides the present value (PV) factor for a particular compounding period (n, which in this case is in years) at the particular compound interest rate.

In the table, you can find the present value factor for 10 years at 10%, which is 0.3855. If we multiply this by the future value of $259.37, we then get the product $99.987, which rounds off to $100 – the present value equivalent of $259.37 ten years from now.

Let's use this principle in another way. Suppose you are now 55, and, late though it may be, you'd want to have a retirement fund of $1,000,000 when you turn 65. The bank offers 10% interest compounded annually. How much should you deposit today and not touch for the next ten years so you could retire with a nest egg of $1,000,000? You calculate:

Calculate: $1,000,000 X 0.3855 =
$385,500

Pretty neat. If you have $385,500 now, and instead of spending it, you deposit it at 10% interest for ten years, then you more than double your money for your retirement. Retirement decisions are very important for everyone, because at some point in the future you will stop working and therefore you won't have any income. Your retirement fund will be the resource that will sustain you. Can you imagine if you began saving at 25 instead of 55?

The time value of money theory follows a convention. Present values are situated one year before your first cash flow if you had a stream of cash flows. The line graph below shows where the present is (Year 0) compared with a series of cash flows whose present values you are calculating.

Figure 6.2 - Line graph for the present value of a stream of cash flows[4]

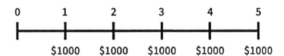

The cash flows are deemed to take place at the end of each year, with no cash flow occurring at Year 0. Just as an exercise, how do we derive the present value of the stream of cash flows shown in the timeline above if the prevailing interest rate is 8%? The solution would look something like this:

Cash Flow	Year	PV Factor (8%)	Present Value B X D
1,000	5	0.6806	680.60
1,000	4	0.7350	735.00
1,000	3	0.7938	793.80
1,000	2	0.8573	857.30
1,000	1	0.9259	925.90
		Total Present Value (Year 0)	3,992.60

The PV factors were lifted from the PV factor table above, for the corresponding interest rate (also called the discount rate) and the corresponding year (or compound period). By multiplying each cash flow by its present value factor, we find the present value for that cash flow. Since all the cash flows have been valued at the present (Year 0), we may now add them to arrive at the present value for the entire series of cash flows.

What does this mean? It means that an installment of $1,000 each at the end of five years is equivalent to a lump sum of $3,992.60 at a discount rate of 8%. If you had the option to receive or make payments either in periodic installments or in one lump sum, you could either opt for five $1,000-yearly cash flows for five years at 8%, or the $3,992.60 lump sum at present. They are of equal value to each other.

Quantifying Intangibles

You will notice that present value calculations are typically used only for tangible costs and benefits that are easily monetized and, therefore, easily compared. Intangible costs and benefits are more difficult, but not impossible, to value in monetary terms. Here are some techniques suggested by Hartman[5] for valuing intangibles.

Scenario Analysis

This process involves evaluating the possible results of performing an activity and estimating the likelihood that an intangible benefit will be received. Based on the odds estimated, a value may be assigned to the intangible benefit. For instance, you have the option of hiring two additional in-house staff to receive client orders or contracting the services of a third-party telemarketing company.

While both options entail the same monetary cost, you estimate from experience that hiring in-house personnel has only a 15% chance of further improving customer satisfaction because hirees off the labor pool are not well-trained to deal with phone-in customers' needs. Calls also tend to pile up during peak hours because the store only has two phone lines.

The professional services of a telemarketing company, however, can improve customer satisfaction by 50% due to the availability of multiple trunk lines and their staff's specialized training in attending to customers' calls. The intangible benefit of contracting a third-party service provider is therefore superior to hiring additional in-house staff.

Process Of Elimination

After a business realizes benefits from an action it has already taken, it may conduct a process-of-elimination analysis to assign a monetary value to that benefit. The company does this by comparing its business performance before and after the measure has been adopted. Suppose XYZ Company decided to streamline its organizational structure. This involved providing a separation pay of $600,000 to personnel it laid off. After the reorganization, profits surged to $1,000,000. The net benefit gained, equal to $1,000,000 less $600,000, or $400,000, is therefore the value of the intangible benefit realized by XYZ as a result of the streamlining effort.

Comparative Analysis

This technique involves comparing the intangible benefit acquired to other similar benefits or intangible assets with fixed values. Comparative analysis is particularly useful in assigning a value to a business's assets in the course of assessing its net worth. Examples of intangible results of past business decisions are assets including customer goodwill, brand names, and patents.

A comparison can be drawn between established intangible assets and similar intangible assets that another company is attempting to sell to a willing buyer. By drawing comparisons and highlighting parallels between the two, it will be possible to make the argument that the unsold, intangible asset is as valuable as another intangible asset sold at a price.

A good analogy could be drawn between the comparative analysis of intangible assets and the valuation of real property. Usually, property values in an area adjust in tandem with the most recent purchases of adjacent real property.

A quick caveat: valuing intangible benefits and costs can never be exact, because of the very nature of intangibles. We may rely on the assessments of experts and predictions by researchers, but these change often as new information emerges. The emergence of new information can make relatively accurate valuations quickly inaccurate. Also, the prior assessment of benefits cannot be guaranteed until it is locked in by an actual monetary transaction or quantifiable results. Even so, the environment changes, so intangible benefits and costs need to be frequently reevaluated to remain relevant.

Weighing The Costs And Benefits

Are all costs and benefits equal to other costs and benefits? One may argue that when they have been valued in monetary terms, then they are proportional or on equal footing and may be directly compared to each other. Mostly, this is so because the dollar is a stable unit of value. That being said, when the cost-benefit analysis aims at maximizing social welfare rather than economic value, analysts employ distributional weights. This involves assigning weights to certain factors to give greater importance to considerations that may help the poor more than the wealthy.

Suppose that you are trying to decide whether you will choose Option A or Option B in the following table. There are tangible costs and benefits, the present values of which are presented. The net tangible benefit is the result of deducting the costs from the benefits, which in this case is the same for the two options. Normally, you would say that Option A has the higher net tangible benefit ($170,000 compared to $140,000) and so should be the solution.

But let's say that an intangible benefit of $100,000 for both options was arrived at by one of the methods in the preceding section. Based on your subjective criteria, you determine that the intangible benefit is slightly more important to you in Option A than in Option B. To reflect this fact, you may assign weights to the benefits. See how this is done in the table below.

	Present value	Weight	Weighted Benefit
Option A			
Tangible Benefit	$ 250,000		
Tangible Cost	80,000		
Net tangible benefit	$ 170,000	30%	51,000
Intangible benefit	100,000	70%	70,000
			$ 121,000
Option B			
Tangible Benefit	$ 220,000		
Tangible Cost	80,000		
Net tangible benefit	$ 140,000	70%	98,000
Intangible benefit	100,000	30%	30,000
			$ 128,000

The weights are assigned as percentages totaling 100% for each option. Intangible benefits are weighted 70% in Option A and 30% in Option B. The net tangible benefits receive a weight equal to the difference between the weights for the intangible benefits and 100%. By multiplying the value of the benefits by their corresponding weights and adding the result, you get weighted benefits that you can compare with each other. In this case, Option B has the greater overall weighted benefit, and your decision should favor this option.

Hypothetical Problem

Suppose you decided to start a hobby that will eventually be run as a not-for-profit corporation. You have many interests: gardening, woodcraft, community service, youth development, animal shelters, and book collection, among others. You determined that this will not primarily be a business for financial profit, but a project that will give you the greatest all-around satisfaction.

Narrowing your choices at this point is a subjective elimination of less probable prospects. Out of those enumerated above, let's say you would forego gardening and woodcraft as less likely choices. Community service and youth development could be symbiotic goals you could combine. But the goals need an activity, which could either be running an animal shelter or creating a library (collecting books).

So, for your cost-benefit analysis, you decide to compare "animal shelter" and "community library." The costs and benefits will be identified from the perspective of the project proponent – you, the proud investor of $5,000, and the youth in the community who are the beneficiaries.

Assuming you had done your research and gathered information on the costs and benefits you will incur for your proposed projects, you would have tabulated your tangible costs and benefits for the two projects according to the format shown in the following two tables. The first table below shows the expected costs and benefits of putting up a community library and running it for the next five years.

Community Library			Years		
	1	2	3	4	5
Costs					
Renovation	5,000				
Computers	15,000		10,000		
Fixtures	5,000				5,000
Furniture	8,000		5,000		
Salaries	36,000	36,000	43,200	43,200	43,200
Book purchases	15,000	8,000	7,000	6,000	5,000
Maintenance & Janitorial	12,000	12,000	12,000	12,000	12,000
Utilities	5,000	5,000	5,000	5,000	5,000
Total Costs	101,000	61,000	82,200	66,200	70,200
Benefits					
Initial donation	60,000				
Pledged donations		20,000	25,000	25,000	25,000
Sponsorships & grants	15,000	15,000	15,000	15,000	15,000
Fundraising	10,000	10,000	10,000	10,000	10,000
Sublease income	24,000	24,000	24,000	24,000	24,000
Total Benefits	109,000	69,000	74,000	74,000	74,000
Net benefits	8,000	8,000	(8,200)	7,800	3,800

The table of projected costs and benefits for the community library shows the cash outflows (costs) and cash inflows (benefits) and their annual totals over the five years. The result of deducting costs from benefits gives us the net benefits shown in the last line of the table. The net benefits are positive (more benefits than costs) for years 1, 2, 4, and 5, while the net benefit is negative for year 3, indicating that costs exceed benefits for that year.

The following table shows the projected cash flows for the costs and benefits of the dog shelter.

Dog Shelter			Years		
	1	2	3	4	5
Costs					
Renovation	5,000				5,000
Kennels	6,000	3,000			
Fixtures	2,000	2,000	2,000		
Salaries	18,000	18,000	20,000	20,000	20,000
Dog food	24,000	28,000	30,000	32,000	34,000
Veterinary fees	6,000	6,000	6,000	6,000	6,000
Medicines & supplies	8,000	9,000	10,000	10,000	10,000
Utilities	5,000	5,000	5,000	5,000	5,000
Totals	74,000	71,000	73,000	73,000	80,000
Benefits					
Initial donation	80,000				
Pledged donations		30,000	30,000	30,000	30,000
Sponsorships & grants	15,000	20,000	25,000	25,000	25,000
Commission income	12,000	15,000	20,000	20,000	20,000
Totals	107,000	65,000	75,000	75,000	75,000
Net benefit	33,000	(6,000)	2,000	2,000	(5,000)

For this project, the net benefits for years 1, 3, and 4 are positive and negative for years 2 and 5.

The next step is to calculate the net present value of the two projects and compare them with each other. The estimated cost of money (or interest rate) is 5%, therefore the PV factors for 5% over the first five years are derived from the table of PV factors shown earlier.

The net benefits for both projects over the five years are assembled in the third and fifth columns. The fourth and sixth columns contain the product of the annual net benefits multiplied by the PV factor. Finally, the sum of the annual present values for each project is shown in the last row of the table.

Year	PV Factor 5%	Library		Shelter	
		Net Benefit	PV	Net Benefit	PV
1	0.9524	8,000	7,619.20	33,000	31,429.20
2	0.9070	8,000	7,256.00	(6,000)	(5,442.00)
3	0.8638	(8,200)	(7,083.16)	2,000	1,727.60
4	0.8227	7,800	6,417.06	2,000	1,645.40
5	0.7835	3,800	2,977.30	(5,000)	(3,917.50)
Total Net PV of Benefits			17,186.40		25,442.70

Comparing the total net present values of the community library and dog shelter, which project has the greater advantage? Purely based on the net present values or NPVs, the better choice is the dog shelter whose net benefit is higher than that of the community library.

There may be instances when alternatives incur costs for us but have no benefits. In such cases, choose the alternative that has lower costs. The general rule is to maximize benefits and minimize costs.

The Need For A Sensitivity Analysis

For some problems, the cost-benefit analysis you conduct from them could be enhanced by a sensitivity analysis. This determines how much of the final net benefit changes if one of the variables it depends on changes – that is, how sensitive the output is to a change in one of the inputs. Sensitivity analysis requires you to make assumptions about the input you wish to study.

In our exercise, note that we stipulated that the interest rate (also known as the discount rate) is 5%. But interest rates change over time, so we might need to know how sensitive our net benefit would be if the discount rate changed. So let us assume that the discount rate changes.

In the next two tables, we present the computation for the net present value of the net benefit, but with the discount rates changed to 2% and 8%, respectively. Note that these two rates are 3% less and more than the original 5%, respectively.

Year	PV Factor 2%	Library		Shelter	
		Net Benefit	PV	Net Benefit	PV
1	0.9804	8,000	7,843.20	33,000	32,353.20
2	0.9612	8,000	7,689.60	(6,000)	(5,767.20)
3	0.9423	(8,200)	(7,726.86)	2,000	1,884.60
4	0.9239	7,800	7,206.42	2,000	1,847.80
5	0.9057	3,800	3,441.66	(5,000)	(4,528.50)
Total Net PV of Benefits			18,454.02		25,789.90
Change from 5% discount rate			7%		1%

Note that there is an additional row below the two tables that shows the change from the 5% discount rate. The two percentages from the right indicate how far each project differs from its net benefit at the 5% discount rate. In the table above, if the discount rate was at 2%, the total benefit is 7% higher for the community library and 1% higher for the dog shelter than they would be if the discount rate was still 5%. In the table below, if the discount rate was at 8%, the total benefit is 6% lower for the community library and 1% lower for the dog shelter than they would be if the discount rate was still 5%.

Year	PV Factor 8%	Library		Shelter	
		Net Benefit	PV	Net Benefit	PV
1	0.9259	8,000	7,407.20	33,000	30,554.70
2	0.8573	8,000	6,858.40	(6,000)	(5,143.80)
3	0.7938	(8,200)	(6,509.16)	2,000	1,587.60
4	0.7350	7,800	5,733.00	2,000	1,470.00
5	0.6806	3,800	2,586.28	(5,000)	(3,403.00)
Total Net PV of Benefits			16,075.72		25,065.50

The net benefits for both projects increase if the discount rate increases, and decrease if the discount rate decreases. We can also observe that for the same change in discount rates, (3% up and down), the net benefits realized from the community library change a great deal more than the net benefits realized from the dog shelter. The value of the total net benefit from the community shelter is therefore more sensitive to changes in the interest rate than the value of the total net benefit from the dog shelter.

What's more, the change in the value of the net benefit from the dog shelter is the same whether the interest rate increases or decreases – the change is only 1% up or down. We can say that the change in value is symmetric vis-a-vis changes in the discount rate. However, the change in the value of the net benefit from the community library is greater when the interest rate goes down (7%), and less when the interest rate goes up (-6%). We can say that the change in value for the community library is asymmetric vis-à-vis changes in the discount rate.

Is it better for the end result – the present value of the total net benefit – to be more or less sensitive to the change in the interest rate? In financial matters, when the swing in possible values is large, analysts view this project as having a higher risk because there is a higher degree of uncertainty. For the community library, the swing is 13% (the difference between 7% and -6%). For the dog shelter, there is a 2% swing (1% to -1%). There is greater certainty in the computed value for the dog shelter than for the community library.

Armed with this extra bit of information, let's go on to decide what to do with the problem.

Making The Decision And Acting On It

The hypothetical problem requires you to decide between putting up a dog shelter and establishing a community library. Based on their tangible present values, and the lower risk that is shown in the sensitivity analysis, you should select the dog shelter.

It is a relief to note that there are tools that can be used to help us assess the financial implications of our decisions. Costs and benefits are quantitative concepts that we must consider if we want to avoid future regrets. The basic math tools in this chapter were explained in some detail so that you may apply them to problems requiring cost-benefit analysis. In all problem-solving situations, just keep the basic principle in mind: try to minimize your costs and maximize your benefits, in whatever form they may be.

Action Steps

Let's see the power of understanding the time value of money in making choices that have financial implications. One real-world problem for many Gen Zers is deciding on what course to take that prepares them for gainful employment.

Dirty Jobs television show host and vocational education advocate Mike Rowe has frequently extolled the comparative benefits of studying for a skilled job versus a college education.[6] Alma, a 12th-grader, read his article and thoughtfully processed its implications for her for the coming school year. She has the option of taking out a student loan and enrolling in Harvard. She heard that obtaining a degree in gender studies is quite popular nowadays. Or she could study to be a welder. Her father works as one, and she heard that there is a shortage of skilled workers in many areas now, welding being one of them.

Alma went online to research the tuition fees and salary structures of the two options. She found out that a year at Harvard can cost as high as $78,200 per year, inclusive of room and board, books, travel expenses, and tuition fees.[7] Alma expects that she may apply for grants and other financial assistance to lower her expenses to (hopefully) $50,000 per year. For a four-year course, her ballpark figures would be $200,000 for the entire program. A viable job for a gender-studies graduate would be a community developer, who can earn as much as $68,000 annually[8] after garnering the necessary experience.

Then Alma researched the viability of becoming a welder. Welding training schools cost anywhere from $5,000 to $15,000 to earn certification.[9] The average expense is $6,850, but Alma decided to go with the upper limit,

$15,000, to get a conservative estimate. The highest-paid welders earn as much as $52,000-$65,000 per year, although some highly skilled welding jobs earn over $100,000.[10] Alma decided to go with a conservative estimate of $48,750 per year[11] for an experienced welder, although she understands that she could make higher than this with overtime pay. The expected annual incomes are spread over seven years, based on the researched data for new entrants (year 1) and experienced practitioners (year 7), and the learning curve anticipated to get from entry to experienced levels.

	Harvard Gender Studies	Vocational Welder
Tuition Fee	200,000	15,000
Income		
Year 1	40,000	30,000
Year 2	54,068	35,000
Year 3	54,068	35,000
Year 4	68,000	40,000
Year 5	68,000	40,000
Year 6	68,000	45,000
Year 7	68,000	48,750

To gain a fair assessment, the incomes are estimated for the first seven years of employment, although they are not simultaneous because training to be a welder is accomplished in a few months, while the college degree is completed only after four years. Working as a welder will commence three years before employment as a community developer, something Alma must keep in mind.

Finally, Alma needed to get a grounded estimate of the expected interest rate. The Financial Times published an article that economists predict the Federal Reserve will keep interest rates above 4% beyond 2023.[12] Armed with this understanding, Alma extracted the following figures from the present value table presented in this chapter.

	PV factor		
	3%	4%	5%
Year			
1	0.9709	0.9615	0.9524
2	0.9426	0.9246	0.9070
3	0.9151	0.8890	0.8636
4	0.8885	0.8548	0.8227
5	0.8626	0.8219	0.7835
6	0.8375	0.7903	0.7462
7	0.8131	0.7599	0.7107

Alma's goal is to be self-sufficient as soon as possible, to ease the financial burden on her parents. She also wants to have as bright a future as possible by investing wisely in her education. Knowing what you do about costs and benefits, could you help Alma think this problem through? You could find the result of the calculations at the end of this chapter.

Moving On

We often think that financial decisions are best relegated to experts, but nothing can be further from the truth. Whether we decide to buy a house or rent a flat, set up a business or seek employment, purchase household needs on cash or credit, take out insurance for ourselves or our property, or save for our retirement, we make deeply personal decisions that cannot be relegated to others. On the other hand, corporations and institutions solve problems using models they develop consistent with their strategies and cultures. We will get to meet some of these models in the next chapter.

Key Takeaways

- Making wise decisions requires that we account for present and future costs and benefits that our decisions will incur for us.
- We must also consider tangible and intangible costs and benefits. Tangible costs and benefits are readily valued in monetary terms. Intangible costs and benefits are more difficult to evaluate and will require methods such as scenario

analysis, the process of elimination, or comparative analysis.

- Costs and benefits may have different levels of importance; therefore, we should assign greater weight to the more important items when making our assessments.
- When choosing between alternatives, we should select the options that provide higher net present benefits, which is the result of deducting the present value of costs from the present value of benefits. The general rule is to maximize benefits and minimize costs.
- When input data tends to vary, conduct a sensitivity analysis around this data to understand how such changes may affect your decision.

Solution To The Exercise In The Action Steps

Alma has all the data she needs to do a present value analysis. Although the interest rate will likely be maintained at 4% according to the Federal Reserve, it would be useful to get present values for 3% and 5% to aid in our estimations. Also, seven years is a useful time span to see short-term trends (5 years may seem too short and 10 years too long).

For Alma's purposes, the present value of costs is just one amount for each option, and that is the tuition fee she expects to spend. Reasonable liberty has been taken in estimating this amount, particularly for the Harvard option since she is assuming the lower limit of the tuition range ($48,000 to $78,000). Although the tuition payments will cover four years, it is reasonable to lump the entire four-year amount into one sum at the beginning. Chances are, she may even exceed this amount.

To get the present values of annual incomes, multiply the estimates by the present value factors in the preceding table. The results are shown in the tables below. Once converted to present values, sum them up to obtain the total present values of the future benefits. Subtract the present value of the costs (the tuition fees) from this sum, and you obtain the net benefit for each option.

Harvard Gender Studies		Present Value of Income		
Duration	Income	3%	4%	5%
Year 1	40,000	38,836	38,460	38,096
Year 2	54,068	50,964	49,991	49,040
Year 3	54,068	49,478	48,066	46,693
Year 4	60,000	53,310	51,288	49,362
Year 5	65,000	56,069	53,424	50,928
Year 6	68,000	56,950	53,740	50,742
Year 7	68,000	55,291	51,673	48,328
Present Values of Benefits		360,898	346,643	333,188
Less: Tuition Fee (Cost)		200,000	200,000	200,000
Net Present Value of Benefit		160,898	146,643	133,188

Vocational Welder		Present Value of Income		
Duration	Income	3%	4%	5%
Year 1	30,000	29,127	28,845	28,572
Year 2	35,000	32,991	32,361	31,745
Year 3	35,000	32,029	31,115	30,226
Year 4	40,000	35,540	34,192	32,908
Year 5	40,000	34,504	32,876	31,340
Year 6	45,000	37,688	35,564	33,579
Year 7	48,750	39,639	37,045	34,647
Present Values of Benefits		241,517	231,998	223,017
Less: Tuition Fee (Cost)		15,000	15,000	15,000
Net Present Value of Benefits		226,517	216,998	208,017

If you were Alma, which option would benefit you more? Becoming a vocational welder has a greater and more immediate reward. You can have the freedom to realize gainful employment sooner and could opt to finance yourself through a subsequent college degree if you wanted.

Remember that if you decide to go immediately to Harvard, you will be taking out a student loan. The payment of this loan includes an interest cost that is not considered in this exercise. The overall cost to you would therefore be considerably larger than we have accounted for here.

7

PROBLEM-SOLVING MODELS AND A PROBLEM-SOLVING PARADIGM

> Stories are like mental flight simulators; they allow us to rehearse problems and become better at dealing with them.[1]
>
> — CHIP AND DAN HEATH

If you've had the same work experiences as I and countless others have had, then you must have changed jobs quite a bit. Every time you join a new company, you would have undergone some sort of orientation by the human resources manager or some similar official. But more than this, you would have relied a lot on the stories your co-workers must have told over lunch or after work.

More than merely gossip, these stories about work give new employees their initial foray into the company culture and how problems are solved there. They also provide current employees a way of exchanging experiences about methods they have found effective.

Is there a single process by which we can solve all our problems? Much as we would like to think so, there is no such process. If we recall Myth #5 in Chapter 4, it says, "A single problem-solving approach fits all types of problems." There is no single approach by which all problems are solved, simply because there are many different types of problems.

Because organizations routinely perform the same activities, they encounter the same type of problems repetitively. The organizations develop standardized procedures to address these problems. In time, successful solutions are adopted as institutionalized models that others in the same industry emulate.

This chapter describes five problem-solving models. We will learn the features that make these models better suited to the types of problems they typically address.

The Analytical Problem-Solving Approach By FEMA

FEMA refers to the Federal Emergency Management Agency. Created by President Jimmy Carter in 1979, it is the principal disaster response unit of the United States. Its headquarters is in Washington, D.C. and it has 10 regional offices located across the country, employing more than 20,00o people nationwide. During major disasters, its workforce can swell to more than 50,000 active members. As of 2003, FEMA became part of the Department of Homeland Security.[2]

As an agency that addresses crises, FEMA naturally would want to standardize its approach to problem-solving to ensure a speedy and accurate response. This is necessary to save lives, prevent casualties, and minimize property damage. It developed the six-step approach, which very closely approximates the traditional 5-step problem-solving process described in Chapter 4. The following figure illustrates the FEMA problem-solving framework.

Figure 7.1 - FEMA's Analytical Problem=Solving Approach [3]

There is one slight difference between the 5-step approach and the FEMA framework. Instead of merely analyzing the problem, the second step in FEMA's approach emphasizes the need to "determine root causes," which extends beyond determining the immediate causes. Amid unfolding disasters, this is a tall order. FEMA employs two special methods of analysis known as the Why Staircase and the Fishbone Diagram.

The Why Staircase is a method of asking and answering a series of dependent questions consecutively about why something occurred. This may be achieved by asking more or less than five questions, but as a general guideline, a set of five questions stands as a rule of thumb. The diagram below illustrates this method.

Figure 7.2 - Discovering the Root Cause: The Why Staircase or the 5 Whys [4]

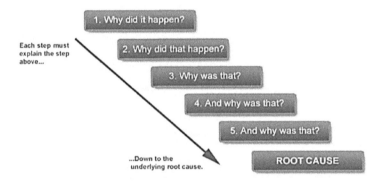

The other method of discovering the root cause of a problem is the cause-and-effect or Fishbone Diagram shown in the next illustration. This technique structures root cause identification while brainstorming. It can also use the results of the Why Staircase to complete the Fishbone Diagram. The visual layout that resembles a fish skeleton helps us analyze whether the issues are closely related (when they are sub-branches of the main category) or discrete factors.

The process begins by creating an outcome statement, shown at the center-right. Follow it up by identifying the major categories of causes that lead to the outcome, which you write as branches from the main arrow. Brainstorm as many causes as you can, and see whether they constitute a new branch, or form part of one of the branches already identified.

Figure 7.3 - Discovering the Root Cause: The Fishbone Diagram [5]

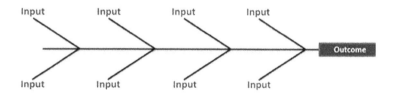

The Ideal Problem-Solving Model

The IDEAL problem-solving model by Bransford & Stein[6] is not ideal in the sense of being perfect or the best problem-solving system. The approach is based on many power ideas the authors combined to create their model. It is designed to help you understand the different parts of problem-solving.

The first step, "Identify" calls us to recognize potential problems as opportunities to do something creative. The second step is to carefully "Define" the goal we wish to achieve. Many times, we recognize the existence of a problem but disagree about what the goal is.

According to Bransford and Stein,[7] a problem exists when an obstacle stands in the way between the present state and the goal state. Sometimes, a problem may be so difficult to solve that we tend to redefine the goal altogether to something that we can achieve. Step 2 requires us to clarify the goal we aim for, and commit to achieving it.

The third step is to "Explore" the alternative ways we may achieve the goal. To do this, we must analyze the problem systematically, dissecting the large problem into simpler components and using our knowledge and reasoning to solve the small parts before putting them together for the larger solution.

The fourth step is to "Anticipate" the possible outcomes and act on them. Anticipating the outcomes helps us to avoid actions that we may regret later on. Testing and using prototypes are typically involved in this step. Finally, "Looking" back and learning allows us to profit from the experience by examining our performance in greater detail. The result is that we are prepared to respond better when we encounter the problematic situation again.

These steps closely approximate the other models, but Bransford and Stein stress one important difference: the five steps are NOT envisioned to be performed in a linear manner, but cyclically or iteratively. You may even perform two steps simultaneously, such as exploring different strategies and at the same time anticipating their outcomes. If upon examining a strategy you realize that it may have undesirable outcomes, you may abandon it and explore other possible strategies.

The Kepner-Tregoe Method

This model is named after its creators, Charles Kepner and Benjamin Tregoe. An important feature of this model is that it disconnects the "problem" from the "decision." The method breaks through the confusion that characterizes the traditional problem-solving pattern that is not sufficient in addressing large problems faced by organizations. It instead distinguishes four rational processes to answer four basic questions.[8]

<u>Situation Analysis – What Is Going On?</u>

This step clarifies the issues surrounding complex situations and structures and prioritizes the related concerns. Management develops plans to effectively resolve each issue identified, the type of analysis required, who needs to be involved, and what particular actions should be taken.

<u>Problem Analysis – Why Did It Happen?</u>

This process seeks to identify the cause of the problem by gathering and analyzing the facts and other information about the problem. The possible causes identified are validated against the facts gathered.

<u>Decision Analysis – What Should We Do?</u>

This activity evaluates a range of alternatives, weighing their relative risks before making a decision. It ensures that management is fully informed regarding maximizing the benefits and minimizing the risks concerning the decision to be made.

Potential Problem Analysis – What Lies Ahead?

This method enables the organization to anticipate threats to the success of its planned solutions. Awareness of potential problems allows management to prepare for contingent actions and identify the triggers to activate them. Management becomes more proactive rather than reactive in addressing the likely issues that arise.

The K-T Problem Solving and Decision-Making method (as the model is also called) is particularly useful to large companies with complex problems. Segregating the problem-solving process isolates and systematizes each step. This allows the problem-solving teams to better troubleshoot and retrace potential missteps that otherwise would have compromised the entire process.

Although the K-T method is designed as an impartial process, it is not immune to personal biases influencing the activity. Even so, management can rigorously and universally apply the K-T method to most organizational situations. It promotes mutual understanding within an organization and helps explain problems to the various functional units.[9]

The Lean Six-Sigma (DMAIC) Process

If you are familiar with the highly popular Total Quality Management (TQM) approach developed by William Edwards Deming, then you know about the DMAIC process. It comprises five phases – Define (define the problem), Measure (quantify the problem), Analyze (identify the cause of the problem), Improve (implement and verify the solution), and Control (maintain the solution) – and aims to improve existing process problems with unknown causes[10].

Let's first get acquainted with the term Lean Six Sigma. This is a "fact-based, data-driven philosophy of improvement that values defect prevention over defect detection."[11] The quality standard known as Six Sigma quality indicates a process that is well-controlled to be within plus-minus three sigmas (symbolized by the Greek letter Σ which stands for a statistical quantity) from the average or center line in a control chart, and whose requirements or tolerance limits are confined within plus-minus six sigmas from the center line. Thus, Six Sigma is the acceptable quality standard in TQM, which the DMAIC process is geared towards achieving.

The Six Sigma philosophy views all work as processes that are capable of definition, quantification, analysis, improvement, and control. Since processes have inputs and outputs, the DMAIC process stipulates control over the inputs and process stages for the outputs to meet quality control. Observe the flowchart illustrating how DMAIC is undertaken.

Figure 7.4 – The DMAIC Flowchart

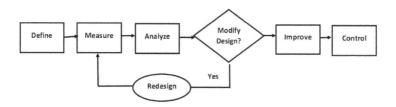

DMAIC is a linear process (unlike the cyclical or iterative processes such as the IDEAL model) that makes use of specialized tools such as statistical process control (SPC), failure mode and effects analysis (FEMA), process mapping, control charts, and others. DMAIC is best applied to project management, production, and engineering. It does not apply to all types of problems.

Technological Method Of Problem Solving

This problem-solving process was adapted from an eighth-grade textbook written for New York State standard technology curriculum. The idea behind its creation is to establish a standard problem-solving procedure to make the process easier and more effective. As it was written for students in the eighth grade, it was intended as a guide to help most people, even adolescents, adopt a systematic method of solving problems.[12] It has seven steps:[13]

1. Describe the problem.

2. Describe the results you want.

3. Gather information.

4. Think of solutions.

5. Choose the best solution.

6. Implement the solution.

7. Evaluate results and make necessary changes.

The process is spiral-shaped, suggesting that this is an iterative, not a linear, process. As an iterative process, you may skip forward or backward on any step of the spiral depending on your progress.

For instance, based on the information you gather (step 3) you might want to redefine the results you want (step 2). Or, as you think of solutions (step 4), you could try tentatively implementing them (step 6) before you go back and choose the best solution (step 5). And so on.

Techniques To Gain A New Perspective

There are times when you find yourself getting into a rut while trying to solve a problem. There are many techniques you could use to gain a fresh point of view. Also, you can get quite creative in devising your own methods. The following are some innovative strategies suggested by Asad Ali[14] in case you get stuck when solving a problem.

Study And Identify The Constraints.

We often jump to intuitively guessing at solutions without first identifying the limitations that constrain or bind us. As a first step remember to always gather complete information and facts about the problem's constraints. This step is most helpful, particularly since most decision problems are constraint satisfaction problems. It will also save you time and effort in later steps of the decision process.

Abstract Away Parts Of The Problems.

One of the best ways to solve problems is to look for analogies. This is done by abstracting the key ideas of the actual problem and creating a model problem that provides us with a fresh perspective. By solving the model problem, we discover an abstract solution that we could apply to the actual problem. The abstract solution could be later converted to a general solution for similar problems we may encounter later.

Solve A Simple Problem And Build Heuristics.

Heuristics, we may recall, are mental shortcuts of "rules of thumb" we instinctively create to simplify problems and avoid cognitive overload.[15] While heuristics are not always guided by logic, they help solve small, simpler parts of the larger problem. By first solving smaller parts, we could build heuristics and rules that will aid us in solving the larger parts. Eventually, we would have created a heuristic for the entire problem, which would be useful should we encounter a similar problem in the future.

Solve The More Constrained Part First.

We might view a problem with constraints as more difficult to solve. On the contrary, as the number of constraints increases, the solution space narrows, possibly to the point of reaching a solution faster.

A familiar example to many would be the popular television show, *Wheel of Fortune*. The contestants select several letters that may or may not form part of a mystery phrase. The presence or absence of the letter becomes a clue to the phrase they are supposed to guess. Each letter becomes a constraint; the more letters appear on the board, the narrower the possible solution set. Words with more letters guessed (i.e., more constraints) are faster to solve first before turning to the words with fewer letters.

The board below has nearly all but a few letters filled in. If no letters were filled in, there is an infinite number of word combinations possible. At this point, the answer can be narrowed down to two possible solutions: "Choosing the right word" and "Choosing the right card." So the more constraints, the easier the solution.

Figure 7.10 - Wheel of Fortune game board[16]

<u>Some Plan Is Always Better Than No Plan.</u>

The 19th-century German field marshal, Helmuth Moltke (also known as Moltke the Elder) believed that it was better to develop several options for battle rather than having a single plan. His famous saying was, "No plan of operations extends with certainty beyond the first encounter with the enemy." Today people[17]remember the saying, "No plan survives contact with the enemy," suggesting that we may be devoting too much time and effort to a plan that fizzles away at the first try.

In practice, it is better to have a plan than no plan at all. Plans are useful even in uncertain situations because it gives you a starting point. All problem-solving is iterative when there are unknowns because we repeatedly go back to check our constraints which may be in flux. We modify and adjust the baseline plan which is superseded with new plans. So, the baseline plan serves its purpose as a springboard for what may come next.

Divide And Conquer.

When a problem is too large, the best approach is typically to divide it into subproblems and solve each subproblem separately. You can do this by having a single team work through the subproblems sequentially, or assigning different teams to each subproblem and assembling the parts to form the final solution.

The divide-and-conquer approach is often used in computer programming and systems design, but it is also applicable in everyday life. When a large family prepares for the traditional Thanksgiving or Christmas reunion, family members typically assign who prepares which dishes for the holiday feast. A complex project in the workplace is divided into strategic segments, each of which is executed by the team with the proper specialized skills. The large undertaking which can be overwhelming therefore becomes manageable when broken down into smaller parts.

Reduce The Problem.

Large problems may be broken into smaller problems, but also consider if all the components are really necessary to solve. At times, a large, complicated problem can be simplified with a change in perspective. Rachel Lim, who was months away from graduating from Nanyang Technological University in Singapore, was stressed by the prospect of juggling school and her fledgling but promising business.[18] Realizing that while she handled both, she excelled in neither, Rachel resolved to simplify her problem from: "How could I succeed in my studies and my business?" to "Which choice should I focus on?" She decided that her business meant more to her than her degree. Today, she is a co-founder of Love, Bonito, a multimillion-dollar global fashion enterprise and one of Southeast Asia's leading online retailers.[19]

Always Look For Analogies

We already discussed how abstracting a problem involves analogies. Aside from this, it is also possible to use analogies in converting a problem encountered for the first time into a familiar form or a related problem where a standard solution already exists. The following is an example of drawing an analogy with a familiar situation.

The story of John Nash, who discovered the Nash Equilibrium, was depicted in the 2002 Academy Award winner for Best Picture, *A Beautiful Mind*. The Nash equilibrium is a revolutionary theory in the mathematics of social interaction. It later found important applications in a wide range of disciplines from economics to the social sciences For this achievement, Nash was awarded the 1994 Nobel Prize in Economics.[20]

In the movie, Nash, played by Russell Crowe, was mulling over the problem of his doctoral thesis as a graduate student at Princeton in 1950. He observed a group of beautiful girls in a bar where he and his classmates were hanging out. All the girls were brunette except for one blonde. The beautiful blonde is the first choice all the boys wanted to approach. But Nash reasoned that if they all went for the blonde, none of them would win her because they would block each other off. After they had been spurned, the natural recourse would be for each of them to go after the brunettes; but none of the brunettes would have wanted to be a second choice after the blonde, so the boys would all be turned away.

The situation inspired Nash to devise the game theory for which he is now famous. The situation at the bar is an analogy of a game, where the boys are players. The actions they may take are strategies, which in this case is either to "go for the blonde" or "go for a brunette." So, given the foregoing situation, the game theory would recommend that none of the boys should "go for the blonde." Instead, each of them should "go for the brunettes" so that each one of them ends up with a partner.[21]

Strategic interaction among the players affects the outcome of the game. The goal is to find the optimum strategy wherein each of the players tries to decide what the others would do, and on this basis selects the best action that will produce optimum results. Nash claims (in the movie, at least) that game theory debunks Adam Smith's dictum, "in competition, individual ambition serves the common good," i.e., everyone goes for the blond girl. The Nash equilibrium produced more practical results in real-world reasoning, that is, in competition, the optimal strategy anticipates the actions of the other players in the game.

The Problem-Solving Paradigm

There is indeed no one way to solve all or even most problems. But there appear to be enough commonalities among the various methods that a generalized framework may be construed that bring these shared factors together. A search through academic literature revealed one problem-solving paradigm that accomplishes just that, the Problem-Solving Paradigm (PSP) proposed by

Bagayoko, Kelley, and Hasan[22] and published in the journal *College Teaching*.

The authors' goal in creating this conceptual framework was to provide students with a tool for academic problem-solving, although the paradigm is just as valid for real-life problems. They note that the two types of problems differ in the degree to which they are defined. Academic problems are clearly defined while real-life problems are more obscure. This paradigm is relevant to both.

The five categories that comprise the paradigm are the bases that determine our proficiency in solving problems. These are:[23]

Knowledge Base

This refers to knowledge that is organized in a condensed and meaningful way, in contrast to sets of disjointed pieces of information. We cannot correctly and consistently apply information that we do not know critically and meaningfully.

Skill Base

This also refers to cognitively condensed knowledge, but of a procedural nature. Although distinct, knowledge in the skill base overlaps somewhat with the knowledge base described above. The skill base refers to the physical or mental dexterity required to solve a problem. In mathematics, for instance, cognizance of differential calculus formulas forms part of the knowledge base but understanding how to solve it belongs to the skill base.

Resource Base

This refers to the pool of human and material resources necessary for the solution. The nature of this base varies significantly with the type of problem being solved. The typical academic problem requires calculators, computer hardware and software, reference books and online sources, as well as subject authorities.

Strategy Base

This covers the strategies and experiences needed to solve the problem. This should not be confused with the skill base. The skill base refers to the capabilities of individual people like the instrument players in an orchestra, in which case the strategy skill would be represented by the conductor of the orchestra who coordinates the players.

Behavioral Base

The affective domain of the problem-solving process. Knowledge, skills, resources, and strategies alone are not sufficient to solve a problem. The right individual reactions to different constraints, such as strong focus and composure, will preclude incidents such as panic attacks and indecision.

The problem-solving paradigm is not a process. It is useful, however, in obtaining a bird's eye view of complex organizational structures or set-ups that are designed to solve problems such as the models described in this chapter. Awareness of the various bases supporting problem-solving proficiency helps managers identify areas in their organization that may be further enhanced to improve their decision-making performance.

Action Steps

Two of the techniques for gaining a new perspective involve creating analogies. Analogies are direct comparisons between two things. In problem-solving, the helpful analogy is between the problem situation in which we have developed a closed mindset and a parallel context that is simpler and more familiar.

This challenge involves matching workplace problems with analogous situations. Part A describes the problem. Part B lists contexts we are all familiar with. The challenge is to match each item in Part A with an item in Part B. There are more items in Part B than in Part A, so you won't be able to rely on simple elimination to match all items together.

You could check your best answers against the answer key at the end of the chapter.

Part A:

1. The Organizational Structure. This is usually comprised of one leader at the top of the company, some supervisors at the middle tier, and many workers comprising the rank-and-file.

2. Mergers And Acquisitions. This involves the process of combining two companies into one, or one large company taking over and absorbing a smaller company.

3. Human Resources Development. This organizational function manages the interpersonal relationship between employees and the company or among the employees with each other. It also enables employees to realize their potentials and ambitions.

4. Complaints And Grievances. The function that threshes out conflicts between employees and management or between two or more employees.

5. Competitive Strategies. This refers to the strategies implemented by management for the company to better address and outperform its competitors in the marketplace. It includes producing better goods and services to score greater customer satisfaction points.

Part B:

I. Court of law conducting a hearing

II. Team sports such as basketball or football games

III. Hannibal Lecter

IV. Pyramid at Giza

V. Family life

VI. A tree with branches and leaves

VII. Marriage

Moving On

Organizations create institutionalized problem-solving models to standardize their responses to recurring problems. As the business environment around them changes, organizations should allow their models to evolve to keep them relevant and updated. In the final chapter, you will find some advice that will help you through whatever problems you may face.

Key Takeaways

- Problem-solving models are systematic methods developed by institutions, organizations, or movements to address the types of problems they regularly encounter.
- The more structured problem-solving methods include the FEMA model for disasters, the DMAIC model for measurable quality management, and the Kepner-Tregoe model which is designed for large organizations with complex problems that need deconstruction and delegation.

- The more intuitive problem-solving methods include the IDEAL and Technological Models. They apply to a broad range of amorphous problems.
- In nearly all problems, the solver must be able to view the problem in a more detached manner and employ creativity that requires a fresh perspective. Eight techniques were identified to achieve this.
- The Problem-Solving Paradigm (PSP) presents a systematic concept for proficient problem-solving.

Answer Key To The Challenge

1. The hierarchical organizational structure is analogous to the classical pyramid, so the answer is IV or the Pyramid at Giza. It is narrow at the top and gradually increases in width on the

way down. The base, like the rank and file, has the greatest width.

2. Mergers and acquisitions (M&A), where (at least) two become one, is like a marriage (VII). The terms of the M&A must be acceptable to all parties concerned or the union will fail. Some may say that mergers are like marriage, but not acquisitions where one party dominates. Actually, in some cultures where marriages are arranged and the male is dominant, the marriage is still very much an acquisition.

3. Human resource development (HRD) is akin to family life (V). The HR department is in charge of job satisfaction, organizational culture, skills development, and harmonious employee relations. In a family, the parents are in charge of family harmony, the children's education and development, the transmission of social values, and the children's happiness.

4. Complaints and grievances can only be likened to hearings in a court of law (I). Many issues that are the subject of

grievances and complaints have legal implications. Parties contend for rights that they feel were transgressed. There are counsels or advocates on both sides, and an impartial tribunal that sits to render judgment.

5. Competitive strategy formulation is analogous to team sports games (II). The key term is competition. Business companies compete against rival companies that provide the same or similar goods and services. The rewards they vie for are increased sales and profits, much like points in the game. The better the performance, the greater the rewards.

The above match-ups leave two unmatched Part B items. The tree (VI) is also a valid analog to organizational structure. A single trunk, management, supports branches and leaves, the smaller units in an organization. So if you matched the tree with organizational structure, this still merits a point.

How about Hannibal Lecter (III)? If you have had a bad experience with mergers and acquisitions, particularly in a hostile takeover, then you might be tempted to compare the act of one large company swallowing or dismembering a smaller and more helpless company to cannibalism. But only if you held a particularly deep-seated grudge from your own M&A experience.

8

SOME FINAL TIPS

> In giving advice seek to help, not to please, your friend.[1]
>
> — SOLON, 638-558 B.C.

The preceding chapters have equipped us with useful inclusions to our problem-solving toolbox. Let us round off the new ideas we have garnered with a few tips to help us convert theories to practice more effectively. Here are a few suggestions.[2]

Keep Calm And Don't Panic

When faced with challenges, particularly those that appear to be dire, our first impulse is to panic. We cannot help it. The arousal of fear is a survival instinct built into our psyche. Uncertainties threaten us. To quell the fear, address the uncertainty. Know that you can immediately take the first of the five steps, which is to understand the problem. Research, read, ask, and think of the options open to you. An immediate calm should descend on you as you realize you have control over the situation.

Don't Jump To Conclusions

Let's be clear: Your first action is to think, not act on impulse. Panic will force us to act out of control without thinking. When we are not thinking clearly, we rush to irrational conclusions. To preclude this, arm yourself with hard facts and evidence that will support your assumptions. Do not jump from Step 1 to Step 5 – go through the intervening steps where you gather information, analyze them, and set up your options. Only then should you decide and take action.

Be Wary Of Problem-Solving Bias

Remember step two? That's when we analyze the problem. We typically resort to reason and logic, but sometimes our analysis is clouded by personal biases that derail our logic. There are many types of biases. Here are four of them.

Overconfidence bias is a tendency to overestimate our abilities and skills. You might be the best tennis player in your club, leading you to mistakenly believe that you are unbeatable anywhere. Unfortunately, you are eliminated in the first round of a regional tournament. But you refuse to acknowledge that you did not prepare well for it, and would rather think that you were cheated.

Confirmation bias is the tendency to interpret new evidence in a manner that affirms our existing beliefs or convictions. If you were raised to believe in the supernatural, you might tend to believe claims of ghostly or spiritual encounters even before investigating whether or not they are backed by objective evidence.

The *bandwagon effect* is our tendency to do something mainly because other people are doing it, regardless of our own beliefs.

The *halo and horn effect* is the "cognitive bias that causes you to allow one trait, either good (halo) or bad (horn), to overshadow other traits, behaviors, actions, or beliefs."[3] It is when our first impression of somebody or something colors our subsequent perception of that person or thing. If you were the recruiting manager in your firm and an applicant struck you as slovenly during his first interview, you might not be inclined to hire him even though he has other positive qualities.

These are only a few biases that could prevent us from making sound decisions. We should be keen on spotting and avoiding them to make better choices.

Take A Break

Ever had the feeling that you had spent hours deeply immersed in analyzing a problem but appeared to be getting nowhere? I have some strange advice for you: Let go. Get off your chair, go to the kitchen and have a snack, or don your sports shirt and slacks and jog around the block. Watch an episode of your favorite Netflix series. Take a break, and do something entirely unconnected with the problem you are trying to solve.

The remedy to dig yourself out of a rut is to open yourself to some random stimulation. *Random stimulation* is a concept developed in the 1960s by Maltese inventor Edward de Bono. It is an important part of lateral thinking, whereby we open ourselves to a variety of information.[4] Even when asleep, we consolidate information and memories that enable us to learn and even discover solutions to problems.[5]

Take the case of German organic chemist August Kekulé. The empirical formula for benzene, a flammable chemical and natural constituent of crude oil, was generally known. However, nobody had yet determined its highly unsaturated structure. In 1865, as Kekulé puzzled over this problem, he stopped writing and dozed off. In his dream, he saw atoms whirling around before his eyes. The atoms then assembled themselves into long rows that slithered around like a snake. As he watched mesmerized, the snake then coiled around and swallowed its own tail. Upon waking, Kekulé realized that the dream held the answer to the elusive molecular structure. He is now credited with the discovery of the benzene's alternative double-bond structure.

Figure 8.1 - August Kekulé, the dream, and the benzene molecule[6]

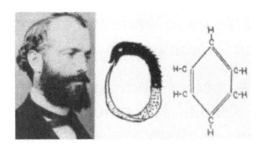

The next time that you meet repeated failure while trying to solve a problem, allow your mind to relax and meander off to nowhere in particular. You might find the answer when you least expect it

might find the answer when you least expect it.

Try The Six Thinking Hats

Finally, before we commit ourselves to a conclusion, we ought to try wearing Edward de Bono's six thinking hats. This is a way of investigating an issue from different viewpoints in a clear and conflict-free manner.[7] The summary table below will give you some insight into the model.

Figure 8.2 - Summary Table: Six Thinking Hats [8]

HAT	APPROACH
WHITE	Facts and Information
RED	Emotion and Intuition
BLACK	Risks and Negatives
YELLOW	Optimism and Positives
GREEN	Creativity and New Ideas
BLUE	Management and Control

The model gives us the advantage of breaking out of any particular mindset that constrains us. By changing hats, we gain fresh perspectives on the problem and become more competent in making balanced decisions. Individuals and groups may move out of habitual ways of thinking and arrive at a more constructive consideration of the decision before adopting it.

Action Steps

Let's play Six Thinking Hats. Here's the storyline.

You were flying your twin-engine Cessna 414 light plane over the Bermuda Triangle when out of the blue, lightning struck your wing, forcing you to crash-land on the ocean. Fortunately, there was a small island nearby which you did not notice on the maps as you charted your flight. You made it to the island on floating debris, armed with the emergency solar high-powered global positioning system (GPS) transmitter that you switched on immediately upon landing on the beach.

Suddenly, a small group of natives emerged from the jungle dressed in loin cloths, with painted faces and crude nose bones, and carrying spears and daggers. They took you to their village where you surmised, after seeing a pile of skulls neatly arranged under a tree, that they were cannibals.

The tribal chief appeared at the entrance of his hut with a beautiful, exotic woman. The tribe's medicine man, who happened to graduate from Harvard Medical School and knew English, explained to you that the beautiful woman, named Marahuyo, is the chief's only daughter.

The chief ominously grunted an order which the medicine man, with a sly wink, translated verbatim as: "Marry Marahuyo before the next full moon, or you will become our guest-of-honor in the full moon feast."

You instantly thought of your wife and three grown children in Los Angeles. The next full moon is one month away. You have only two clear options:

1. Marry Marahuyo.

2. Do not marry Marahuyo.

Everything else about your future actions – what you will do, how and when you will do them, what you will tell the chief and the medicine man – are open for you to plan out and determine.

Using the six thinking hats, what will you do?

Moving On

The pieces of advice given in this chapter are meant to help you, although you are probably familiar with them already. That does not mean you always remember to observe them because, in the urgency of the moment, you may panic, jump to conclusions, and render a biased judgment. Just remember, when you are at your wit's end, take a break. And use the six hats.

Key Takeaways

- When solving problems, keep calm with the knowledge that you are in control of the situation.
- Avoid jumping to conclusions; follow the five steps of problem-solving to ensure that you don't overlook anything important.
- Beware of the different biases, particularly overconfidence bias, confirmation bias, the bandwagon effect, and the halo and horn effect.
- When you appear to be going nowhere, take a break. Random stimulation may lead you to new ideas and possibly even the solution to your problem.
- Adjust your perspective by trying the Six Thinking Hats.

.

Ingram Content Group UK Ltd.
Milton Keynes UK
UKHW021125180423
420361UK00014B/844